At Issue

Guns: Conceal and Carry

Other Books in the At Issue Series

At Issue

| Guns: Conceal
and Carry

Anne Cunningham, Book Editor

GREENHAVEN
PUBLISHING

Published in 2018 by Greenhaven Publishing, LLC
353 3rd Avenue, Suite 255, New York, NY 10010

Articles in Greenhaven Publishing anthologies are often edited for length to meet page
requirements. In addition, original titles of these works are changed to clearly present
the main thesis and to explicitly indicate the author's opinion. Every effort is made to
ensure that Greenhaven Publishing accurately reflects the original intent of the authors.
Every effort has been made to trace the owners of the copyrighted material.

Cover image: AVN Photo Lab/Shutterstock.com

Library of Congress Cataloging-in-Publication Data

Names: Cunningham, Anne C., editor.
Title: Guns: conceal and carry / edited by Anne C. Cunningham.
Description: New York : Greenhaven Publishing, 2018. | Series: At Issue | Includes
 bibliographical references and index. | Audience: Grades 9-12.
Identifiers: LCCN ISBN 9781534500624 (library bound) | ISBN 9781534500600
 (pbk.)
Subjects: LCSH: Firearms--Law and legislation--United States--Juvenile literature. |
 Gun control--United States--Juvenile literature.
Classification: LCC KF3941.G867 2018 | DDC 344.730533--dc23

Manufactured in the United States of America

Website: http://greenhavenpublishing.com

Contents

Introduction

Americans have an abiding and emotional relationship with guns. The option to keep a gun for hunting or self-defense is a constitutionally protected and deeply cherished right, but does this mean that gun owners should be permitted to bring their guns to any public space, at any time? Are laws banning guns from sensitive areas such as schools and government buildings constitutional and in the public interest? Should states require concealed weapon permit seekers to demonstrate a compelling reason why they wish to carry a gun, and if so, what reasons qualify as valid? These and other similarly thorny questions pertaining to "concealed carry" comprise an especially controversial subset of contemporary gun law and policy. Indeed, experts such as Joseph Blocher, from whom we will hear in the pages that follow, identify concealed carry as the most important field within the larger debate over gun rights and restrictions.

The purpose of this book is to examine the concealed carry debate from a variety of angles and viewpoints. It includes articles representing a wide range of ideological and political positions. Some writers advocate virtually unfettered rights to carry concealed weapons. Others present anecdotal and statistical evidence to the contrary, supporting common sense limits on where gun owners can take their weapons for the sake of public safety. If we step back and view this discussion from a more general perspective, the debate over concealed carry reveals familiar tradeoffs between individual liberty and the public good. Since vastly different interpretations emerge as to how best to balance these prerogatives, an in-depth understanding of multiple perspectives on the concealed carry issue is crucial to reaching an informed position.

Despite daily reports of injuries and fatalities by firearms, to say nothing of the brutal spate of high profile mass shootings in recent years, majority support for gun rights in this country remains steadfast. According to recent opinion polls conducted by Pew Research Center, 52% of those surveyed wish to protect the right to own a gun absolutely. By contrast, only 46% support new restrictions on gun ownership. This divide is starkly polarized politically. 79% of Democrats support gun control measures, while a staggering 90% of Republicans favor broad gun rights with minimal restrictive legislation. Some bipartisan support exists for "common sense" gun laws including universal background checks, a ban on assault weapons, and restrictions for those on federal terror watch and no fly lists from owning guns. Contrary to the desires of the co-called no compromise gun lobby, this indicates that Americans share common ground regarding the impact of widespread gun availability on public health and safety.

Dating back to 1791, the Second Amendment of the U.S. Constitution provides a foundational text for gun rights advocates. It is supported by the majority of the population, and is unlikely to see repeal. Nonetheless, this amendment is both brief and notoriously vague, and has therefore been subject to varying interpretation over the years. Moreover, even legal scholars disagree over how precisely to interpret the provision for "a well-regulated Militia" given the obvious differences between late eighteenth century America and today's highly professionalized and technologically powerful military.

In the landmark 2008 case *District of Columbia v. Heller*, the Supreme Court ruled 5-4 that "the right of the people to keep and bear Arms" protects the individual's right to own a gun, rather than any collective right to form militias. Although the court ruled conclusively that citizens are permitted to own guns for traditional reasons such as sport and self-defense, the decision also contained a carefully worded statement that the Second Amendment does not confer a "right to keep and carry any weapon whatsoever in any manner whatsoever and for whatever purpose." Thus, under the *Heller* decision, states would be free to establish gun-free zones, prohibit felons and the mentally ill from purchasing guns, or enact any other "presumptively lawful" legislation restricting firearm access and use.

Once the Supreme Court turned firearm regulations over to the states, a lively and sometimes fierce debate over the details ensued. As usual, the NRA and others in the extreme pro-gun camp advocated for as little restriction as possible. Even in the face of horrific mass shootings, their argument is always that having more "good guys" with guns is beneficial for society. The logic is that criminals will always ignore the law and carry an illegal gun anywhere they wish. Thus, if more law-abiding citizens are potentially carrying concealed weapons in public, this will deter violent crime. Leading proponents of this viewpoint such as John R. Lott Jr. defend this assertion by citing a statistically insignificant number of accidental shootings by concealed weapon permit holders, and a great many reported instances in which gun owners have thwarted a possible crime, though the exact number and specific circumstances of these cases has been contested.

Even granting this argument a certain superficial clarity, many Americans remain uncomfortable with the prospect of an armed public of would-be vigilantes. Most Americans believe that schools, college campuses, and other sensitive public sites should remain gun free zones. In the aftermath of the 2012 mass shooting at Sandy Hook Elementary, some on the pro-gun side used the tragedy to argue for the abolition of these zones. Those opposing this view countered that even in the unlikely event that an armed civilian could prevent or mitigate a shooting event, the role of educators is to teach and be role models, and not to become a de facto security force. On college campuses, where the use of alcohol is frequent, the presence of a concealed firearm could cause a situation to escalate and become fatal. For these reasons, only 17 states currently allow concealed carry in public institutions of higher education.

Presently, the majority of states maintain restrictions on who can carry a concealed weapon, with most populated states of New York and California having the toughest restrictions. These states have what is called a "may issue" stance toward concealed weapons.

In other words, an applicant must prove a threat of danger to receive a permit. This raises difficult questions as to what constitutes a legitimate threat. States adopting a more lenient stance towards concealed weapons are said to be "shall issue" states. In this case, only a felony conviction or mental illness is grounds for denial. A small number of states have no permit requirements whatsoever, but these tend to be sparsely populated states such as Vermont.

It is expected that gun legislation will migrate to the state, county, and municipal levels, while some observers believe the trend is moving towards less restriction overall. However, what is likely to happen is bifurcation: liberal states will pass tougher gun control measures, while conservative states will gut any remaining restrictions on guns. States are said to be the laboratory of democracy. As such, perhaps these experiments may help guide public policy on guns in a way that reduces violent crime and accidental deaths and injury.

1

Guns Will Affect Classroom Interactions

Jonathan M. Metzl

Jonathan Metzl is the Director of the Center for Medicine, Health, and Society at Vanderbilt University and Research Director of the Safe Tennessee Project. His books include The Protest Psychosis, Prozac on the Couch, and Against Health: How Health Became the New Morality.

Across the United States, colleges and universities are granting permission for instructors and students to bring firearms into classrooms. This is a change even for universities that previously allowed open carry on campus. The distinction is that guns were not allowed into the classroom. But now, prompted by several tragic high-profile campus shootings, administrators and lawmakers have changed the rules in an effort to make campuses safer. But will it? Some people believe it will not. And worse, they caution that the presence of firearms in the classroom will have unintended negative effects, like hampering free discussions.

M issouri is poised to become the latest state to allow guns into college classrooms.

The Republican-led state senate is currently finalizing deliberations on a bill that, if passed, would remove restrictions on carrying concealed weapons on college campuses statewide.

"Are Looser Gun Laws Changing the Social Fabric of Missouri?" by Jonathan M. Metzl, The Conversation, March 11, 2015. https://theconversation.com/are-looser-gun-laws-changing-the-social-fabric-of-missouri-55800. Licensed under CC BY-ND 4.0 International.

The specter of loaded firearms in college classrooms raises particular concerns in no small part because the dynamics of learning often depend on professors challenging students to step beyond their comfort zones.

But beneath these concerns lies a broader question: do guns change the ways that people engage with each other?

Scholars who research guns and gun violence, myself included, often track the impact of guns through homicide and injury rates. But the impact of guns on everyday interactions, and instances when guns are neither drawn nor discharged, remains a largely unstudied topic.

So I decided to talk to people about it. I'm a native Missourian, and I went back home for research as part of a book project about guns in everyday life. Last month I interviewed 50 people, including everyday citizens, religious and political leaders and gun-violence prevention advocates in Kansas City, Columbia and St. Louis about the impact new guns laws are having on social interactions in the state.

Again and again, people with whom I spoke raised concerns, not just about the lethal potential of firearms, but about the ways that allowing guns into previously gun-free communal spaces might impact a host of commonplace civic encounters as well.

Missouri Used to Have Some of the Strictest Gun Laws in the Country

Missouri used to have among the strictest gun laws in the nation, including a requirement that handgun buyers undergo background checks in person at sheriffs' offices before obtaining gun permits.

But over the past 10 years, an increasingly conservative legislature and citizenry relaxed limitations governing practically every aspect of buying, owning and carrying guns. The legislature relaxed prohibitions on the concealed and open carry of firearms in public spaces, lowered the legal age to carry a concealed gun from 21 to 19 and repealed many of the requirements for comprehensive background checks and purchase permits.

And in 2014 voters approved Amendment 5 – which effectively [negated] the rights of cities or towns to pass or enforce practically any form of gun control.

A Natural Experiment

What followed was a state of affairs that *The New York Times* has described as a "natural experiment" testing whether more guns led to more safety and less crime.

Instead, according to research, the opposite occurred, in as much as gun deaths soared when it became easier for people to buy and carry firearms.

A team of researchers led by Daniel Webster, director of the Johns Hopkins Center for Gun Policy and Research, analyzed extensive crime data from Missouri and found that the state's 2007 repeal of its permit-to-purchase handgun law "was associated with a 25 percent increase in firearm homicides rates." Between 2008 and 2014 the Missouri gun homicide rate rose to 47 percent higher than the national average.

Missouri's startling rates of gun death made national news. At the same time, many people with whom I spoke – and particularly people who did not support recent legislative developments – suggested that loosening gun laws also forced nonarmed citizens to adapt in ways that ranged from acceptance to anxiety to avoidance.

Heightening Racial Tensions

For instance, a number of African Americans I interviewed worried that guns heightened racial tensions.

I met a man named John Steen who now thinks twice about shopping at Sam's Club. Steen, a Vietnam veteran who works in Kansas City, used to stop by the wholesale megastore on his way home from his job as a home health-care provider. But that was before he saw armed white men strolling through the aisles exerting what gun proponents describe as their "unalienable" rights to carry firearms into public spaces including retail stores.

For Steen and other African Americans in Kansas City, the result was often intimidation. "I see white guys and their sons walking around Sam's Club, Walmart, and other places where we shop, strolling with guns on their hips like it's the wild west," he told me. "They're trying to be all macho, like they have power because of their guns, walking down the aisles. It just makes me… stay away."

Subverting the traditional narrative of racial anxiety, African Americans often cited the charged implications of white citizens brandishing guns in mixed race settings – a narrative that played out writ large in downtown St. Louis after the passage of Amendment 5 and just months before protests began in nearby Ferguson when white Missouri open-carry advocates paraded through the streets waving handguns, long guns and assault rifles.

For Rev. Dr. Cassandra Gould, events such as these illustrate a double standard through which society codes white gun owners as "protectors" and black gun owners as "threats."

As Pastor of Quinn Chapel A.M.E. Church in Jefferson City, Gould led an intense debate among her congregants after the shooting in Charleston, South Carolina in June 2015 that yielded a decision to ban guns in their house of worship. For Gould, "even though I want us to be protected, I can't escape the fact that these are the same guns that are oppressing communities of color in our state."

Accidental Shootings Are Up

The complexities of parenting in a milieu surrounded by firearms emerged as another theme.

In Missouri there are now virtually no remaining laws governing gun safety or storage. And the state now leads the nation in accidental shootings by toddlers – instances where young children find unlocked guns and accidentally discharge them.

In response, the Missouri chapter of Moms Demand Action signed onto a BeSmart campaign promoting safety steps including training parents to secure guns in their homes and ask about proper firearm storage before dropping children off at a friend's house.

As Becky Morgan, Missouri Chapter Lead for Moms puts it when we spoke, "this is a new step to parents are taking to look out for our children's safety. We already ask about food allergies, pet allergies and pools. Now we ask if firearms are in the home, are they stored properly out of children's reach?"

"I've seen people with guns in their belts at the supermarket," a Columbia parent named Megan White added. "It makes me reconsider bringing my kid on shopping trips."

Caution surrounds a host of everyday interactions as well. Consultant Jeff Fromm thinks about armed motorists when he drives to and from work in downtown Kansas City. "I try not to drive too close to other cars on the highway, or pass in front of anyone at a stoplight. Road rage takes on a whole new meaning when you don't know who's going to be armed."

Changing the Fabric of Social Interactions?

Thoughts about gun proliferation even impact exchanges in the halls of power that passed gun legislation on the first place.

Democratic Missouri State Representative Stacey Newman worries that many legislators and their staff carry concealed weapons during heated debates on the House floor.

"With new laws, capital security can no longer ask lawmakers to check their firearms at the door," she explained. "And I often find it quite unnerving that the people I'm working with or arguing against might well be carrying secret guns during our legislative sessions."

To be sure, notions of an armed society are precisely what many pro-gun-rights Missourians and legislators envision and support.

John L., an advertising consultant who asked that his last name not be used, told me that he appreciates being able to carry a concealed firearm when he visits printing factories and other work sites. "I've been robbed before," he explained. "The thought that I can carry a gun just makes me feel safer."

Linda Hopkins, owner of Smokin' Guns BBQ in North Kansas City, told me that she welcomes customers who carry concealed weapons and feels far more angered by "food prices and intrusive government regulations."

For these and other reasons, *Guns and Ammo* magazine recently cited Missouri as "ahead of the curve when it comes to gun rights" and a "top state for gun owners" thanks in large part to legislation allowing concealed carry.

But a number of Missourians with whom I spoke felt otherwise. Their concerns seemed to provide broader context for questions of civic engagement, power relations, and conflict resolution that lie at the core of debates about allowing guns into college classrooms. And more broadly, the experiences of Missourians suggest a need for more research into ways that allowing guns into the public sphere might impact otherwise quotidian social interactions.

Newman, the state representative, particularly worries about the effect that guns will have on the "psyches of our children" who go to college to learn and grow in a safe environment, and instead may soon encounter classrooms where guns and armed confrontations remain "constant possibilities." For Newman, the issue hit home when her daughter enrolled in grad school at the University of Missouri in Kansas City. "As a parent this is my worst nightmare."

Meanwhile Steen, the home health provider, has seen enough of guns in his lifetime. "I was in Vietnam with the U.S. military, I saw what it means to draw a gun and shoot another person, it's devastating. Trust me…most of these people have no idea."

2

Concealed Weapons Should Be Allowed On Campus

Michael Newbern

Michael Newbern is Legislative Affairs Committee Chair of the Republican Liberty Caucus of Ohio and Ohio Director and National Spokesperson for Students for Concealed Carry.

A recent study published by the Johns Hopkins Center for Gun Policy and Research concluded that concealed weapons on college campuses would increase gun violence. Arguing against this conclusion, Michael Newbern, spokesperson for Students for Concealed Carry, counters that more "good guys with guns" would prevent or mitigate crime. Newbern claims the Johns Hopkins study is flawed, and does not meet peer-review standards. Newbern's own analysis of 17 colleges in the seven states that allow for concealed weapons finds no data supporting a correlation between concealed carry and higher rates of gun violence on campus.

An October 15 report by Daniel W. Webster, director of the Johns Hopkins Center for Gun Policy and Research, and nine coauthors has resulted in several bold headlines but little critical analysis. Articles with titles such as "Report: Allowing Guns On Campus Results In More, Not Less, Gun Violence" and "Guns on campus unlikely to increase safety, study finds" belie both the fact that the report is theoretical and doesn't cite any resulting

"Johns Hopkins Report on Concealed Carry is Seriously Flawed," By Michael Newbern, Students for Concealed Carry, November 1, 2016. Reprinted by permission.

gun violence on college campuses and the fact that the report, which involved no data analysis and was neither published nor peer-reviewed, is not actually a "study" in the academic sense of the word.

At best, the report is a pedantic, overly verbose op-ed that attempts to couch the usual arguments against campus carry in academic language. At worst, it is an attempt to portray the work of two of Dr. Webster's coauthors—John Donohue and Louis Klarevas—as "the best available research" (p.2) on the subject of licensed concealed carry.

Propaganda doesn't become research just because it's written on letterhead from a prestigious university. If these ten professors genuinely wanted to study the issue, they could have conducted a peer-reviewed meta-analysis of the existing literature. Instead, they chose to phone it in with an editorial touting only those outlier studies that reinforce their personal prejudices.

Those of us leading SCC are merely undergraduates and are, therefore, unequipped to prepare a formal academic analysis of a report authored by ten doctors. We are, however, more than equipped to point out flawed logic, straw man arguments, and factual errors.

The Report in Question

Claims, "The Most Recent Rigorous Research Studies Find RTC Laws Linked to Increased Violence" (p. 16), but cites only the prior work of report coauthor John Donohue and ignores the fact that Donohue's findings are contradicted by the preponderance of peer-reviewed research on the subject, including a more recent (2015) study by Charles D. Phillips, Regents Professor of health and policy management at the Texas A&M School of Public Health. Dr. Phillips' study concluded:

> The basic question underlying the hypotheses investigated in this research is simple—Is CHL licensing related in any way to crime rates? The results of this research indicate that no such relationships exist. For our study states, during the time

period covered by our data, changes in crime rates did not affect subsequent CHL licensing rates. In addition, CHL licensing rates did not have a significant, negative or positive, effect on subsequent crime rates.

Hypothesizes, "Increasing gun availability in campus environments could make far more common acts of aggression, recklessness, or self-harm more deadly and, thus, have a deleterious impact on the safety of students, faculty, and staff" (p. 3), but fails to examine the experiences of campuses that already allow licensed concealed carry.

The University of Texas at Austin's campus carry policy working group, which was tasked with researching the issue of campus carry prior to the enactment of Texas' campus carry law, found no reports of resulting assaults or suicide attempts at campus-carry colleges and stated:

> We reached out to 17 research universities in the seven campus-carry states...Most respondents reported that campus carry had not had much direct impact on student life or academic affairs...What we can say is that we have found little evidence of campus violence that can be directly linked to campus carry, and none that involves an intentional shooting...We found that the evidence does not support the claim that a causal link exists between campus carry and an increased rate of sexual assault. We found no evidence that campus carry has caused an increase in suicide rates on campuses in other states.

Focuses heavily on rebutting claims that campus carry will make college campuses safer and that active shooters seek out gun-free zones, despite the fact that such claims are not ubiquitous in the campus carry movement and are eschewed by Students for Concealed Carry, the nation's leading campus carry advocacy group.

Claims, "According to the advocates of allowing civilians to carry firearms on college campuses, some individuals considering perpetrating a mass shooting will be deterred from attacking places where they stand a likelihood of being confronted by private citizens carrying firearms. In instances when deterrence fails and attacks are initiated, campus-carry advocates claim that armed students and staff will be able to intervene and halt gun rampages and thereby minimize the number of victims killed or wounded in the attack" (p. 7). The report backs up this attribution of motive by linking not to a policy paper by a pro-campus carry organization or to a speech by a pro-campus carry politician but, rather, to a listicle titled "12 Times Mass Shootings Were Stopped by Good Guys With Guns," on the website ControversialTimes.com.

Claims, "Advocates for allowing civilians to bring guns onto college campuses and to deregulate carrying of guns in public places in general commonly cite research and statements by John Lott, an economist widely known for his claims that deregulating gun possession reaps significant reductions in violent crime" (p. 8). As proof that advocates generally rely on Dr. Lott's work to make the case for campus carry, the report offers only a couple of endnotes citing Dr. Lott's "More Guns, Less Crime" series of articles and books.

An examination of SCC's Common Arguments page, SCC's 2015 Texas legislative handout, and SCC's 2015-2016 Texas press releases (three documents that if combined and published in book form would be the approximate length of *The Adventures of Tom Sawyer*) reveals only this one reference to the research of Dr. John Lott:

> According to one gun-rights research group, there have been "only two mass public shootings since at least 1950 that have not been part of some other crime where at least four people have been killed in an area where civilians are generally allowed to have guns." This source obviously isn't unbiased, and they admit to having looked only at "public shootings…where the point of the attack is simply to kill as many people as possible," but this finding combined with the relatively low rate of licensure during the 2000-2013 period does give us reason to believe that maybe—just maybe—it's unreasonable to assume that CHL holders would have been directly involved (not just somewhere nearby) in a large number of active-shooter incidents.

Offers the John Lott/David Mustard ("More Guns, Less Crime") studies as the primary counterargument to the report's position but ignores harder-to-rebut conflicting research such as the 2015 Phillips study cited above.

Argues (p. 22) that campus carry would impede campus law enforcement but fails to examine the impact of licensed concealed carry on law enforcement in non-collegiate environments.

Argues, "Most campus officers routinely respond to situations in which information is sparse. They respond to calls such as 'suspicious person,' 'suspicious circumstances,' '911-hang up,' and 'alarm sounding' often with no additional information. If the presence of guns must be assumed, the level of seriousness, tactics used, and necessary precautions taken in response to such calls are elevated" (p. 23). However, in the absence of metal detectors, X-ray machines, or any other screening measure designed to prevent criminals from bringing guns onto campus, officers on any open campus—even a "gun-free" campus—must assume the presence of guns.

When officers get a report of a suspicious person, they don't approach the suspect, thinking, "We'd better be careful—this guy might have passed extensive state and federal background checks in order to obtain a license to carry a handgun." They're thinking, "We'd better be careful—this guy might be a criminal who doesn't care what the law says about carrying a gun or shooting a police officer."

States, "A recent study identified 85 incidents of shootings or undesirable discharges of firearms on college campuses in the U.S. from January 2013 through June 2016" (p. 3). This suggests that the authors of the report anticipate no difference in the behavior of individuals who endure personal expense and an extensive vetting process to obtain the right to lawfully carry a handgun on campus and those individuals who currently choose to ignore the school policies and state laws prohibiting possession of firearms on campus.

States, "Research demonstrates that access to firearms substantially increases suicide risks, especially among adolescents and young adults, as firearms are the most common method of lethal self-harm" (p. 3). However, the report offers no explanation as to how campus carry could increase the risk of student suicide if it doesn't change the ability of a student to own a gun; have a gun at home, where 90% of suicides occur; or—in many states, including Texas—keep a handgun in a locked automobile parked on campus.

Claims, "Binge drinking, a common behavior among college students, especially elevates risks for involvement in violent altercations" (p. 3), but fails to note that most student drinking (particularly binge drinking) takes places at college parties and that most college parties take place at private residences where licensed concealed carry is already legal.

The 2011 study "Drinking at college parties: Examining the influence of student host-status and party-location" found that 84.5% of college party hosts lived off-campus.

The 2015 study "Not Just Fun and Games: A Review of College Drinking Games Research From 2004 to 2013" found that 65% of drinking games are played at private homes (14% at bars) and that "first-year college students reported being more likely to drink in gaming environments with a small gathering of friends at a private residence."

The types of locations where students are likely to consume alcohol are seldom the types of locations affected by campus gun bans and are, therefore, unlikely to be affected by campus carry laws. Texas' campus carry law, which took effect on August 1, 2016, did not change the laws at fraternity houses, bars, tailgating events, or off-campus parties—none of which were covered by the nullified gun ban.

Cites (p. 19) numerous studies on the brain development of teenagers, as an argument against allowing campus carry by adults age 21 and above.

The report fails to mention that Jay N. Giedd, M.D., the author of five of the cited studies on adolescent brain development, also wrote:

> Late maturation of the prefrontal cortex, which is essential in judgment, decision making and impulse control, has prominently entered discourse affecting the social, legislative, judicial, parenting and educational realms. Despite the temptation to trade the complexity and ambiguity of human behavior for the clarity and aesthetic beauty of colorful brain images, we must be careful not to over-interpret the neuroimaging findings as they relate to public policy.

It should be noted that when scientists say that the human brain does not fully mature until the age of 25, the emphasis is on the word "fully." The vast majority of brain development is completed by age 20. The remaining development is, in essence, finishing touches. Saying that the brain of a 21-year-old is not fully developed is like saying that a construction crew hasn't finished building a house, simply because they still haven't put the covers on the light switches—the statement is technically true but highly misleading. There is little or no scientific evidence that the decision making ability of a 21-year-old is substantially or even measurably different from that of a 25-year-old. However, there is a good deal of scientific evidence to the contrary.

Argues, "Age-specific homicide offending peaks around the age when youth reach the minimum legal age for purchasing, and carrying handguns (19-21 years)" (p. 3) and, "Risks for violence, suicide attempts, alcohol abuse, and risky behavior are greatly elevated among college-age youth" (p. 24). However, the report neglects to examine state-level data on the rates of concealed handgun license (CHL) revocation among persons of typical college age.

According to statistics from the Texas Department of Public Safety, 0.147% of CHL holders between the ages of 18* and 23 had their licenses revoked in 2015. For those age 21-23, the 2015 revocation rate was 1.50%. By comparison, 0.155% of license holders between the ages of 38 and 43 had their concealed handgun licenses revoked that year.

*A person age 18-20 can only obtain a Texas CHL if he or she is a member or veteran of the U.S. Armed Forces. As of January 1, 2016, there were a maximum of 333 active Texas CHLs held by military personnel and veterans age 18-20. In that age range, that's approximately one Texan out of every 3,634, or 0.0275%.

Conflates (p. 2) mass shootings (which typically happen in private residences and involve domestic disputes) and public rampage shootings, to reinforce the report's assertion that most shooting sprees happen where civilians are allowed to have guns.

Reinforces its assertion that concealed handgun license holders consistently fail to stop mass shootings, by noting, "A review conducted by [report coauthor Louis] Klarevas of the 111 high-fatality mass shootings (six or more victims murdered) that occurred in the U.S. since 1966 found that only eighteen have taken place, in whole or in part, in a gun-free zone or gun-restricting zone" (p. 10). However, that finding is not entirely accurate.

Only thirty (27%) of the cited incidents took place in states that had shall-issue concealed handgun licensing laws at the time of the shooting. (Klarevas lists four Texas shootings that took place pre-1996, when only a law enforcement officer could lawfully carry a handgun in public. He lists fourteen incidents that took place in California, which has very restrictive licensing laws.)

Of those thirty incidents that took place in shall-issue states, sixteen took place entirely in private residences not open to the public. (The authors of this report apparently interpret the case of an Indiana man killing his six children in their sleep as a failure of licensed concealed carry.)

Of the remaining fourteen incidents that took place, in part or in whole, in public spaces, two were shootouts between rival gangs—not the type of threat against which a law-abiding citizen has much need to defend himself or herself and not the type of threat against which one person with a handgun is of much use.

That leaves just twelve incidents (10.8% of the list of 111) for which a case might be made that a concealed handgun license holder could have reasonably and lawfully intervened. And those twelve include two incidents in which the public portion of the shooting involved the gunman firing a rifle from the cover and concealment of an automobile—another scenario that doesn't fit the model of a typical rampage shooting and that doesn't lend itself to armed intervention by a CHL holder.

Offers a footnote (p. 11) listing five mass shootings that purportedly took place in locations where civilians were allowed to possess firearms. That foot note:

Lists the July 7, 2016, Dallas sniper attack, with no mention/ examination of the fact that a sniper attack is logistically and strategically very different from a typical rampage shooting and offers little chance for intervention by a CHL holder.

Lists an attack near Palestine, Texas, that took place on private property.

Lists the Umpqua Community College shooting in Oregon, with no mention/examination of the fact that concealed carry was against school policy for faculty, staff, and students. The report mentions that there were armed students on this campus, despite the fact that there is no record/evidence that there were armed students in the building where the shooting occurred. The only confirmed armed student (who was carrying a handgun in violation of school policy) was in a different building on the same campus and wisely chose to stay put.

Lists the terrorist attack at the Inland Regional Center in San Bernardino, California, despite the fact licensed concealed carry is heavily restricted and relatively rare in California. The report mentions that there were armed civilians on site, despite the fact that there is no record/evidence that there were armed civilians in the building where the shooting occurred. The only confirmed armed civilian was in a building across the street from the Inland Regional Center. He saw one of the suspects fleeing but, not being sure what was happening, wisely chose not to fire.

Notes, "By contrast, the FBI found that 21 of the 160 active shooting incidents were interrupted when unarmed civilians confronted and restrained the gunmen. The FBI's data suggest that unarmed civilians are more than twenty times likely to successfully end an active shooting than are armed civilians" (p. 12). The report fails to note that, of the 21 incidents stopped by unarmed civilians, 11 occurred in schools where concealed carry was not allowed.

Fails to account for the relatively low rate of concealed handgun licensure during the course of the cited studies and for the relative infrequency of public active shooter incidents, both of which make it statistically unlikely that one or more armed license holders were within sight of the gunman or gunmen during a significant number of these active shooter incidents.

Argues, "Shooting accurately and making appropriate judgments about when and how to shoot in chaotic, high-stress situations requires a high level of familiarity with tactics and the ability to manage stress under intense pressure" (p. 11). This argument conflates self-defense with law-enforcement-style interdiction.

The reference to "tactics" suggests that the authors believe that the average license holder, upon finding himself or herself in the vicinity of a mass shooting, would act like an amateur, one-man SWAT team and attempt to single-handedly clear the building and find the assailant or assailants. This is in direct conflict with the self-defense intent of licensed concealed carry and with standard concealed handgun training.

The report ignores the fact that survivors and victims of mass shootings have watched from nearby hiding spots as gunmen reloaded or have spent several minutes corresponding with 911 operators or loved ones before being shot.

The report ignores the fact that mass shootings are not the only or even the most common form of assault on college campuses and that, according to most experts, a shooting is likely to involve an assailant no more than three yards away, last no more than three seconds, and involve no more than three shots fired. In such a scenario, there is little need for "tactics."

Suggests that "allowing more civilians to carry firearms into more public places could also facilitate more mass shootings. The Violence Policy Center has tracked incidents in which a concealed carry weapon (CCW) permit holder was alleged to have committed various crimes of violence and unintentional shootings. They identified 29 CCW holders who perpetrated non -- defensive shootings that involved three or more deaths not including the shooter during the period 2007 -- 2015" (p. 12). The report fails to note that 26 of those incidents clearly had nothing to do with licensed concealed carry, that two of those incidents most likely had nothing to do with licensed concealed carry, and that the one incident that likely related to licensed concealed carry was perpetrated by a convicted felon who should have been disqualified from obtaining a carry permit but was issued one due to a database error.

Concludes by noting, "Concealed carry permit holders have passed criminal background checks and, as a group, commit crimes at a relatively low rate. But, in states with the most lax standards for legal gun ownership, 60% of individuals incarcerated for committing crimes with guns were legal gun owners when they committed their crimes" (p. 23). This odd statement conflates concealed handgun license holders and legal gun owners—two groups that, although there is some minor overlap, are far from one and the same.

Comparing statistics on gun ownership with statistics on concealed handgun licensure suggests that less than 10% of gun owners are licensed to carry a handgun.

In Texas, CHL/LTC holders are convicted of violent crimes at approximately 1/8 the rate of unlicensed adults and account for less than 0.5% of all criminal convictions for violent crimes.

3

Guns In School Do Not Prevent Crime

Evan DeFilippis

Evan DeFilippis graduated from the University of Oklahoma with a triple degree in Economics, Political Science, and Psychology. His work on domestic and international public health has been published in The Atlantic, Slate, Washington Post, VICE, and Huffington Post.

Will allowing concealed guns on school property not prevent shootings? Or will it instead increase violence and confusion? Despite several high profile mass shootings on school grounds, students as a group see comparatively lower rates of gun violence than the rest of the population. Existing data proves this is a function of widespread firearm bans on school grounds. In the wake of mass shootings such as those at Virginia Tech and University of California-Santa Barbara (USCB), the National Rifle Association (NRA) (who always believes that the answer to gun violence is more guns) is seeking the removal of gun restrictions in schools. Although the Second Amendment allows restrictions on guns in certain venues, some states have successfully overturned these bans.

Why Did Chris Die?

After his son Christopher was gunned down near the campus of the University of California, Santa Barbara on May 23, Richard Martinez sounded what has become a famous plea.

"Why did Chris die?" he asked, choking back tears. "Chris died because of craven, irresponsible politicians and the [National

"Campus Gun Control Works—Why Guns and Schools Do Not Mix," by Evan DeFilippis, armedwithreason, June 7, 2014. Reprinted by permission.

Rifle Association]. They talk about gun rights. What about Chris's right to live?" He went on, "When will this insanity stop? . . . We don't have to live like this."

In response to Martinez's impassioned appeal for gun control, the cavalcade of bumper-sticker slogans rolled in—"guns don't kill people, people kill people," "control criminals, not guns," "don't punish law abiding citizens," and so on.

The NRA has been silent on the shooting, as is its usual media strategy following high-profile gun violence. But we know its position: the solution to gun violence is always more guns.

Thus the express goal of the NRA and other pro-gun groups is to promote the concealed carrying of firearms on college campuses. As the NRA puts it, "Colleges rely on colorful 'no gun' signs, foolishly expecting compliance from psychopaths."

To this end, the NRA and state legislators are pushing guns at every level of schooling. The lobby backed a new Indiana law that allows guns on school property, so long as they are contained within parked cars. "Teachers have to leave their 2nd Amendment rights at the front door when they go to work," said Indiana Senator Brent Steele, explaining why he supported the measure, in spite of the fact that the courts have never wavered on the constitutionality of gun bans on school property. A bill in Nebraska, if passed, would allow teachers and school employees to carry concealed handguns in schools. In Idaho Governor Butch Otter recently signed a law that allows residents with "enhanced concealed-carry permits" to keep firearms on college campuses. A similar bill passed a Florida Senate panel but ultimately was voted down.

The consistent refrain from conservative lawmakers and the gun lobby has been that such legislation will enhance security in schools. The logic is that if students and teachers are armed, or at least protected by armed guards, shootings such as those at Columbine High School in 1999, Virginia Tech in 2007, Sandy Hook Elementary School in 2012, UCSB, and, yesterday, Seattle Pacific University, either will not occur or will be less deadly.

Yet the evidence points in the opposite direction. Schools, including college campuses, exemplify the success of gun control. Though our schools are far deadlier than those of other countries with stricter gun control policies, they are safer than other corners of America that lack stringent constraints on guns.

How Safe Is School?

Despite the fact that the United States compares favorably to other high-income nations in terms of school bullying rates, we are the exception in terms of lethal school violence. The most comprehensive study of school shootings to date—encompassing thirty-eight countries between 1764 and 2009—found that the United States had one less mass shooting than all the other countries combined.

The disparity in lethal school violence between the United States and other countries is almost entirely a function of firearm prevalence. It is not a coincidence that, in the United States, the vast majority of mass killings are carried out with a firearm, while in China, which had the second highest rate of mass killings in the dataset, not a single one was carried out with a gun.

But while American schools may be less safe than their international counterparts, they are still among the safest places in the United States.

Among school-age children, less than 1 percent of homicides occur either on school grounds or on the way to school, even though far more than 1 percent of students' time is spent in school and en route. A Justice Department study showed that, between 1995 and 2002, college students between the ages of eighteen and twenty-four experienced 24 percent less violence than non-college students in the same age group. When college students experienced violence, it occurred off-campus 93 percent of the time.

These sanguine statistics are a reflection of the near universal prohibition of firearms by academic institutions. At least thirty-eight states ban firearms on school grounds, and sixteen explicitly prohibit concealed carry on campus. Such policies enjoy massive public support: according to one survey carried out by researchers at the Harvard School of Public Health, 94 percent of Americans feel less safe when fellow citizens "bring their guns into restaurants, college campuses, sports stadiums, bars, hospitals, or government buildings" and "overwhelmingly, the public believes that in many venues gun carrying should be prohibited."

So just what sort of effect would guns on school grounds have? For starters, we can be confident they would not decrease school violence.

Public Carrying Doesn't Reduce Crime

One of the intellectual touchstones behind the pro-gun movement's support for extending concealed carry permits to schools is John R. Lott's book *More Guns, Less Crime*, first released in 1998 and since updated twice. In response to the book's claims, a sixteen-member panel of the National Research Council convened in 2004 to address the relationship between right-to-carry laws and crime rates and concluded that the existing evidence did not support the more guns, less crime hypothesis. A reexamination of the NRC's findings in 2010 found that, at best, concealed carry laws have a negligible effect on crime rates and, at worst, concealed carrying increases rates of aggravated assault. Two legal scholars, Ian Ayres and John Donohue, further reviewed Lott's findings and discovered that his data contain numerous coding and econometric errors that, when corrected, yield the opposite conclusion: right-to-carry laws increase crime. This was the second time Lott presented findings with "convenient" coding errors, and, when confronted by Ayres and Donohue's research, he removed his name from a paper that claimed to confirm his results.

One of the largest and most recent studies on gun violence in America concludes that widespread gun ownership is the driving force behind violence. The study compiles data from all fifty states between 1981 and 2010 to examine the relationship between gun ownership and homicide. After accounting for national trends in violent crime as well as eighteen control variables, the study concludes, "For each percentage point increase in gun ownership the firearm homicide rate increased by 0.9%." This research is consistent with evidence showing that even in "gun utopias" such as Israel and Switzerland, more guns means more violence.

Another large study compared 91 case workplaces with 205 control workplaces and found that workers whose job sites allow guns are about five times more likely to be killed on the job than are those whose workplaces prohibit all firearms.

Given the weight of evidence demonstrating the danger of carrying guns in public settings, it is extremely unlikely that more guns would make schools safer.

Why Allowing Guns on Campus is an Especially Bad Idea

In a recent editorial in the *Chronicle of Higher Education*, former Idaho State University Provost Gary Olson spoke to the realities of firearms on campus, their limited potential to improve safety, and the near certainty that they would have the opposite effect. "There is no recorded incident in which a victim—or spectator—of a violent crime on a campus has prevented that crime by brandishing a weapon," Olson wrote. "In fact, campus police officers report that increasing the number of guns on a campus would increase police problems exponentially, especially in 'active shooter' situations." Ninety-five percent of university presidents share his opposition to concealed carrying on campus.

If we take a sober assessment—one that will be sorely lacking at college keggers—it is not difficult to imagine the ramifications of widespread gun ownership at colleges. Alcohol abuse, bullying and hazing, high population density, and academic stressors are all predictive of violence—and all are ubiquitous on college campuses.

Guns and Alcohol Don't Mix

Thirty-one percent of college students meet the DSM-IV criteria for alcohol abuse, and alcohol is used in 95 percent of violent crimes, 90 percent of rapes, and 66 percent of suicides among college students. Alcohol consumption renders police officers, people trained to use firearms, unfit for duty, so what should we expect from students who lack the preparation and discipline of police officers?

The most recent survey of firearm ownership on college campuses found that gun-owning students are more likely than non–gun owning students to engage in dangerous behavior such as binge drinking and, when inebriated, participate in activities that increase the risk of life-threatening injury to themselves and others. These include drunk driving, vandalism, and physical violence.

Given excessive consumption of drugs and alcohol on campus, the best a college can do is take precautionary measures to minimize the chance that lapses in judgment and drug- or alcohol-induced impulsivity will become lethal in the presence of a firearm. The only way to do this is to prohibit or at least strictly control guns on campus. It is simply not possible for campus police to monitor every party to ensure that those possessing guns are sober enough to do so. In any case, gun control is practically required in light of court rulings that force universities to provide safe premises to residents and visitors. Universities can be held liable for criminal assault on school grounds and for negligence in connection with social life on campus.

It should be obvious that the combination of alcohol abuse and firearms increases the potential for serious violence. After all, the archetypical "rational actor" is painfully sober. On a typical weekend, the average college student hardly fits the profile of a "good guy with a gun" advanced by gun advocates.

Accidents Happen

Even without the presence of alcohol, accidents happen much more often than gun advocates would like to admit. And when accidents happen with guns, they are often deadly. Individuals in households with firearms, for example, are four times more likely to die of accidental death than those in households without firearms.

The NRA supports bills that permit guns to be carried in vehicles on school grounds, arguing that firearm owners should not be punished for accidentally leaving a gun in their car. Curiously, there seems to be little concern for what happens if the same careless owner accidentally forgets to lock his car, accidentally fails to put the safety on, or accidentally pulls the trigger, ad infinitum. It seems clear that there are many more ways to accidentally go wrong with a gun than there are ways to go right, and this is especially true in a densely populated, anxiety-ridden, alcohol-saturated, hormone-fueled school environment.

Guns and Suicide

While suicide is the second leading cause of death among college students, the rate of about 6.5 to 7.5 per 100,000 is roughly half that of a matched non-student population. The difference in suicide rates between student and non-student populations is explained almost completely by the reduced access to firearms on college campuses. Consider that suicides committed with firearms represent only five percent of suicide attempts but more than half of suicide fatalities. About 1,100 college students commit suicide each year, and another 24,000 attempt to do so. Given that suicide attempts with a firearm are successful 90 percent of the time, each one of these more than 25,000 attempts would almost certainly result in death if carried out with a firearm.

The best studies to date show that the majority of suicides are impulsive,with little deliberation prior to the act. We also know that youths between the ages of eighteen and twenty-five experience the highest rates of mental illness in the general population. These factors, combined with high rates of alcohol and drug abuse, provide a compelling reason to believe that the nation's suicide rate will increase if firearms are allowed on college campuses.

Gun Theft

According to a Department of Justice report, between 2005 and 2010, an average of 232,000 firearms were stolen each year, primarily in residential burglaries. In a survey of incarcerated felons, about one-third of respondents report having stolen their most recently acquired handgun.

A dorm room is one of the least secure places to store a firearm. School dormitories are small, cramped, shared spaces, and they receive a large number of visitors. It would be difficult to conceal the fact that a dorm resident owns a firearm; more likely, the student would flaunt this fact. This means it is a lot easier for a thief to identify potential targets and successfully steal a firearm. And once a gun is stolen, it is much more likely to be used in a crime than if it were in possession of its rightful owner.

Armed Students Are Unlikely To Stop Shooters

Even if a student or professor were to confront a shooter, their chances of stopping a bad guy with a gun would be slim. This should be self-evident given that New York City Police, for instance, only hit their target in 18 percent of cases. The average student or professor would likely have a substantially lower hit rate, thereby increasing the threat to innocent bystanders.

A *20/20* segment, "If I Only Had a Gun," showed just how hopeless the average person is in reacting effectively to high-stress situations. In the segment, students with varying levels of firearm experience were given hands-on police training exceeding the level required by half the states in order to obtain a concealed carry permit. Each of these students was subsequently exposed to a manufactured but realistic scenario in which, unbeknownst to them, a man entered their classroom and begin firing fake bullets at the lecturer and students.

In each one of the cases, the reaction by the good guy with a gun was abysmal. The first participant, who had significant firing experience, couldn't even get the gun out of his holster. The second participant exposed her body to the assailant and was shot in the head. The third, paralyzed with fear, couldn't draw his weapon and was shot by the assailant almost immediately. The final participant, who had hundreds of hours of experience with firearms, was unable to draw his weapon and was shot at point blank range.

Stand Your Ground

A recent *New York Times* article, in brilliant tongue-and-cheek, exposes some harrowing prospects that could result from arming college campuses. The author satirically asks if students using laser-pointers in class or arguing over coffee is sufficient cause to fire away. While this may sound absurd, lax gun laws have created shooting scenarios just like this. In recent years, people have been shot over skittles, popcorn, and their choice of music. It is easy to think up a whole laundry list of relatively common occurrences that could provide legal justification to shoot at a student.

Heightening the risk of needless bloodshed, the states most likely to push for guns on campuses often have stand-your-ground laws as well. As Judge Debra Nelson told jurors in the trial of George Zimmerman for the killing of Trayvon Martin, Zimmerman "had the right to stand his ground and meet force with force, including deadly force if he reasonably believed that it was necessary to do so to prevent death or great bodily harm to himself or another or to prevent the commission of a forcible felony." In other words, in a stand-your-ground state, authority to end another person's life rests with one's own perceptions and convictions, with all their attendant biases. In a high-stress environment such as college, where rationality can be sorely lacking in dangerous moments, the presence of a gun can only make the situation worse, and stand-your-ground laws provide ample room to shoot first and justify later.

Back to School

You are in college. You show up at a fraternity party late one weekend. You don't know much about those attending, except that some may be carrying a firearm due to a new policy permitting concealed carry on campus. Do you feel more or less safe knowing that some of the party attendees may be armed and intoxicated?

If you are like 94 percent of Americans, you feel less safe knowing that people in your community carry guns into public spaces such as colleges. But we need not rely only on the public's expressed preferences when it comes to gun control in schools. The evidence is clear. While gun advocates complain that control measures don't work, the case of our schools—and workplaces—stands as a sharp rebuke: where guns are carefully controlled, there is less gun violence. And where young people are most vulnerable to heavy drug and alcohol use, accidents, theft, poor judgment, and impulsive behavior, more guns won't mean less crime but more mayhem.

4

Concealed Weapons Deter Crime

John R. Lott, Jr.

John R. Lott Jr. has held positions at the University of Chicago, Yale University, Stanford, UCLA, Wharton, and Rice, and was the chief economist at the United States Sentencing Commission during 1988 and 1989.

Many experts contend that concealed weapons reduce crime. While gun control can be an emotional issue, there does exist data to support arguments. How that data is used, however, can make a difference, and can confuse the issue. Some critics counter that introducing a concealed weapon into a violent confrontation increases the likelihood that someone will die. But cross-sectional and time-series data on the county level between 1977 and 1992 may not support this. One study notes over 400,000 instances in which a permitted weapon owner believes having a gun "almost certainly" saved a life. This data can be used to press for "shall issue" laws, and claims "1,570 murders and over 4,177 rapes" could be prevented by such measures, with little change to the rate of accidental firearm death.

Abstract

Using cross-sectional time-series data for U.S. counties from 1977 to 1992, we find that allowing citizens to carry concealed weapons deters violent crimes and it appears to produce no increase in accidental deaths. If those states which did not have right-to-carry concealed gun provisions had adopted them in 1992, approximately

"Crime, Deterrence, and Right-to-Carry Concealed Handguns," by John R. Lott, Jr. and David B. Mustard, Cathedral and the Bazaar, July 26, 1996. Reprinted by permission.

1,570 murders; 4,177 rapes; and over 60,000 aggravate assaults would have been avoided yearly. On the other hand, consistent with the notion of criminals responding to incentives, we find criminals substituting into property crimes involving stealth and where the probabilities of contact between the criminal and the victim are minimal. The largest population counties where the deterrence effect on violent crimes is greatest are where the substitution effect into property crimes is highest. Concealed handguns also have their greatest deterrent effect in the highest crime counties. Higher arrest and conviction rates consistently and dramatically reduce the crime rate. Consistent with other recent work (Lott, 1992b), the results imply that increasing the arrest rate, independent of the probability of eventual conviction, imposes a significant penalty on criminals. The estimated annual gain from allowing concealed handguns is at least $6.214 billion.

I. Introduction

Will allowing concealed handguns make it likely that otherwise law abiding citizens will harm each other? Or, will the threat of citizens carrying weapons primarily deter criminals? To some, the logic is fairly straightforward. Philip Cook argues that, "If you introduce a gun into a violent encounter, it increases the chance that someone will die."[1] A large number of murders may arise from unintentional fits of rage that are quickly regretted, and simply keeping guns out of people's reach would prevent deaths.[2] Using the National Crime Victimization Survey (NCVS), Cook (1991, p. 56, fn. 4) further states that each year there are "only" 80,000 to 82,000 defensive uses of guns during assaults, robberies, and household burglaries.[3] By contrast, other surveys imply that private firearms may be used in self-defense up to two and a half million times each year, with 400,000 of these defenders believing that using the gun "almost certainly" saved a life (Kleck and Gertz, 1995, pp. 153, 180, and 182-3).[4] With total firearm deaths from homicides and accidents equaling 19,187 in 1991 (Statistical Abstract of the United States,

1995), the Kleck and Gertz numbers, even if wrong by a very large factor, suggest that defensive gun use on net saved lives.

While cases like the 1992 incident where a Japanese student was shot on his way to a Halloween party in Louisiana make international headlines (Japan Economic Newswire, May 23, 1993 and Sharn, *USA TODAY*, September 9, 1993), they are rare. In another highly publicized case, a Dallas resident recently became the only Texas resident so far charged with using a permitted concealed weapon in a fatal shooting (Potok, March 22, 1996, p. 3A).[5] Yet, in neither case was the shooting found to be unlawful. [6] The rarity of these incidents is reflected in Florida statistics: 221,443 licenses were issued between October 1, 1987 and April 30, 1994, but only 18 crimes involving firearms were committed by those with licenses (Cramer and Kopel, 1995, p. 691).[7] While a statewide breakdown on the nature of those crimes is not available, Dade county records indicate that four crimes involving a permitted handgun took place there between September 1987 and August 1992 and none of those cases resulted in injury (pp. 691-2).

The potential defensive nature of guns is indicated by the different rates of so-called "hot burglaries," where residents are at home when the criminals strike (e.g., Kopel, 1992, p. 155 and Lott, 1994). Almost half the burglaries in Canada and Britain, which have tough gun control laws, are "hot burglaries." By contrast, the U.S., with laxer restrictions, has a "hot burglary" rate of only 13 percent. Consistent with this, surveys of convicted felons in America reveals that they are much more worried about armed victims than they are about running into the police. This fear of potentially armed victims causes American burglars to spend more time than their foreign counterparts "casing" a house to ensure that nobody is home. Felons frequently comment in these interviews that they avoid late-night burglaries because "that's the way to get shot."[8]

The case for concealed handgun use is similar. The use of concealed handguns by some law abiding citizens may create a positive externality for others. By the very nature of these guns being concealed, criminals are unable to tell whether the victim is armed before they strike, thus raising criminals' expected costs for committing many types of crimes.

Stories of individuals using guns to defend themselves has helped motivate thirty-one states to adopt laws requiring authorities to issue, without discretion, concealed-weapons permits to qualified applicants.[9] This constitutes a dramatic increase from the nine states that allowed concealed weapons in 1986.[10] While many studies examine the effects of gun control (see Kleck, 1995 for a survey), and a smaller number of papers specifically address the right-to-carry concealed firearms (e.g., Cook, et al., 1995; Cramer and Kopel, 1995; McDowall, et. al., 1995; and Kleck and Patterson, 1993), these papers involve little more than either time-series or cross-sectional evidence comparing mean crime rates, and none controls for variables that normally concern economists (e.g., the probability of arrest and conviction and the length of prison sentences or even variables like personal income).[11] These papers fail to recognize that, since it is frequently only the largest population counties that are very restrictive when local authorities have been given discretion in granting concealed handgun permits, "shall issue" concealed handgun permit laws, which require permit requests be granted unless the individual has a criminal record or a history of significant mental illness (Cramer and Kopel, 1995, pp. 680-707), will not alter the number of permits being issued in all counties.

Other papers suffer from additional weaknesses. The paper by McDowall, et. al. (1995), which evaluates right-to-carry provisions, was widely cited in the popular press. Yet, their study suffers from many major methodological flaws: for instance, without explanation, they pick only three cities in Florida and one city each in Mississippi and Oregon (despite the provisions involving statewide laws); and they neither use the same sample period nor the same method of picking geographical areas for each of those cities.[12]

Our paper hopes to overcome these problems by using annual cross-sectional time-series county level crime data for the entire United States from 1977 to 1992 to investigate the impact of "shall issue" right-to-carry firearm laws. It is also the first paper to study the questions of deterrence using these data. While many recent studies employ proxies for deterrence -- such as police expenditures or general levels of imprisonment (Levitt, 1996) -- we are able to use arrest rates by type of crime, and for a subset of our data also conviction rates and sentence lengths by type of crime.[13] We also attempt to analyze a question noted but not empirically addressed in this literature: the concern over causality between increases in handgun usage and crime rates. Is it higher crime that leads to increased handgun ownership, or the reverse? The issue is more complicated than simply whether carrying concealed firearms reduces murders because there are questions over whether criminals might substitute between different types of crimes as well as the extent to which accidental handgun deaths might increase.

II. Problems Testing the Impact of "Shall Issue" Concealed Handgun Provisions on Crime

Starting with Becker (1968), many economists have found evidence broadly consistent with the deterrent effect of punishment (e.g., Ehrlich (1973), Block and Heineke (1975), Landes (1978), Lott (1987), Andreoni (1995), Reynolds (1995), and Levitt (1996)). The notion is that the expected penalty affects the prospective criminal's desire to commit a crime. This penalty consists of the probabilities of arrest and conviction and the length of the prison sentence. It is reasonable to disentangle the probability of arrest from the probability of conviction since accused individuals appear to suffer large reputational penalties simply from being arrested (Lott, 1992b). Likewise, conviction also imposes many different penalties (e.g., lost licenses, lost voting rights, further reductions in earnings, etc.) even if the criminal is never sentenced to prison (Lott, 1990b, 1992a and b).

While this discussion is well understood, the net effect of "shall issue" right-to-carry, concealed handguns is ambiguous and remains to be tested when other factors influencing the returns to crime are controlled for. The first difficulty involves the availability of detailed county level data on a variety of crimes over 3054 counties during the period from 1977 to 1992. Unfortunately, for the time period we study, the FBI's Uniform Crime Report only includes arrest rate data rather than conviction rates or prison sentences. While we make use of the arrest rate information, we will also use county level dummies, which admittedly constitute a rather imperfect way to control for cross county differences such as differences in expected penalties. Fortunately, however, alternative variables are available to help us proxy for changes in legal regimes that affect the crime rate. One such method is to use another crime category as an exogenous variable that is correlated with the crimes that we are studying, but at the same time is unrelated to the changes in right-to-carry firearm laws. Finally, after telephoning law enforcement officials in all 50 states, we were able to collect time-series county level conviction rates and mean prison sentence lengths for three states (Arizona, Oregon, and Washington).

The FBI crime reports include seven categories of crime: murder, rape, aggravated assault, robbery, auto theft, burglary, and larceny.[14] Two additional summary categories were included: violent crimes (including murder, rape, aggravated assault, and robbery) and property crimes (including auto theft, burglary, and larceny). Despite being widely reported measures in the press, these broader categories are somewhat problematic in that all crimes are given the same weight (e.g., one murder equals one aggravated assault). Even the narrower categories are somewhat broad for our purposes. For example, robbery includes not only street robberies which seem the most likely to be affected by "shall issue" laws, but also bank robberies where the additional return to having armed citizens would appear to be small.[15] Likewise, larceny involves crimes of "stealth," but these range from pick pockets, where "shall issue" laws could be important, to coin machine theft.[16]

This aggregation of crime categories makes it difficult to separate out which crimes might be deterred from increased handgun ownership, and which crimes might be increasing as a result of a substitution effect. Generally, we expect that the crimes most likely to be deterred by concealed handgun laws are those involving direct contact between the victim and the criminal, especially those occurring in a place where victims otherwise would not be allowed to carry firearms. For example, aggravated assault, murder, robbery, and rape seem most likely to fit both conditions, though obviously some of all these crimes can occur in places like residences where the victims could already possess firearms to protect themselves.

By contrast, crimes like auto theft seem unlikely to be deterred by gun ownership. While larceny is more debatable, in general __ to the extent that these crimes actually involve "stealth" __ the probability that victims will notice the crime being committed seems low and thus the opportunities to use a gun are relatively rare. The effect on burglary is ambiguous from a theoretical standpoint. It is true that if "shall issue" laws cause more people to own a gun, the chance of a burglar breaking into a house with an armed resident goes up. However, if some of those who already owned guns now obtain right-to-carry permits, the relative cost of crimes like armed street robbery and certain other types of robberies (where an armed patron may be present) should rise relative to that for burglary.

Previous concealed handgun studies that rely on state level data suffer from an important potential problem: they ignore the heterogeneity within states (e.g., Linsky, et. al., 1988 and Cramer and Kopel, 1995). Our telephone conversations with many law enforcement officials have made it very clear that there was a large variation across counties within a state in terms of how freely gun permits were granted to residents prior to the adoption of "shall issue" right-to-carry laws.[17] All those we talked to strongly indicated that the most populous counties had previously adopted by far the most restrictive practices on issuing permits. The implication for existing studies is that simply using state level data rather than county data will bias the results against finding any impact from passing right-to-carry provisions. Those counties that were unaffected by the law must be separated out from those counties where the change could be quite dramatic. Even cross-sectional city data (e.g., Kleck and Patterson, 1993) will not solve this problem, because without time series data it is impossible to know what impact a change in the law had for a particular city.

There are two ways of handling this problem. First, for the national sample, we can see whether the passage of "shall issue" right-to-carry laws produces systematically different effects between the high and low population counties. Second, for three states, Arizona, Oregon, and Pennsylvania, we have acquired time series data on the number of right-to-carry permits for each county. The normal difficulty with using data on the number of permits involves the question of causality: do more permits make crimes more costly or do higher crimes lead to more permits? The change in the number of permits before and after the change in the state laws allows us to rank the counties on the basis of how restrictive they had actually been in issuing permits prior to the change in the law. Of course there is still the question of why the state concealed handgun law changed, but since we are dealing with county level rather than state level data we benefit from the fact that those counties which had the most restrictive permitting policies were also the most likely to have the new laws exogenously imposed upon them by the rest of their state.

Using county level data also has another important advantage in that both crime and arrest rates vary widely within states. In fact, as Table 1 indicates, the standard deviation of both crime and arrest rates across states is almost always smaller than the average within state standard deviation across counties. With the exception of robbery, the standard deviation across states for crime rates ranges from between 61 and 83 percent of the average of the standard deviation within states. (The difference between these two columns with respect to violent crimes arises because robberies make up such a large fraction of the total crimes in this category.) For arrest rates, the numbers are much more dramatic, with the standard deviation across states as small as 15 percent of the average of the standard deviation within states. These results imply that it is no more accurate to view all the counties in the typical state as a homogenous unit than it is to view all the states in the United States as one homogenous unit. For example, when a state's arrest rate rises, it may make a big difference whether that increase is taking place in the most or least crime prone counties. Depending upon which types of counties the changes in arrest rates are occurring in and depending on how sensitive the crime rates are to changes in those particular counties could produce widely differing estimates of how increasing a state's average arrest rate will deter crime. Aggregating these data may thus make it more difficult to discern the true relationship that exists between deterrence and crime.

Perhaps the relatively small across-state variation as compared to within-state variations is not so surprising given that states tend to average out differences as they encompass both rural and urban areas. Yet, when coupled with the preceding discussion on how concealed handgun provisions affected different counties in the same state differently, these numbers strongly imply that it risky to assume that states are homogenous units with respect to either how crimes are punished or how the laws which affect gun usage are changed. Unfortunately, this focus of state level data is pervasive in the entire crime literature, which focuses on state or city level data and fails to recognize the differences between rural and urban counties.

However, using county level data has some drawbacks. Frequently, because of the low crime rates in many low population counties, it is quite common to find huge variations in the arrest and conviction rates between years. In addition, our sample indicates that annual conviction rates for some counties are as high as 13 times the offense rate. This anomaly arises for a couple reasons. First, the year in which the offense occurs frequently differs from the year in which the arrests and/or convictions occur. Second, an offense may involve more than one offender. Unfortunately, the FBI data set allows us neither to link the years in which offenses and arrests occurred nor to link offenders with a particular crime. When dealing with counties where only a couple murders occur annually, arrests or convictions can be multiples higher than the number of offenses in a year. This data problem appears especially noticeable for murder and rape.

One partial solution is to limit the sample to only counties with large populations. For counties with a large numbers of crimes, these waves have a significantly smoother flow of arrests and convictions relative to offenses. An alternative solution is to take a moving average of the arrest or conviction rates over several years, though this reduces the length of the usable sample period, depending upon how many years are used to compute this average. Furthermore, the moving average solution does nothing to alleviate the effect of multiple suspects being arrested for a single crime.

Another concern is that otherwise law abiding citizens may have carried concealed handguns even before it was legal to do so. If shall issue laws do not alter the total number of concealed handguns carried by otherwise law abiding citizens but merely legalizes their previous actions, passing these laws seems unlikely to affect crime rates. The only real effect from making concealed handguns legal could arise from people being more willing to use handguns to defend themselves, though this might also imply that they more likely to make mistakes using these handguns.

It is also possible that concealed firearm laws both make individuals safer and increase crime rates at the same time. As Peltzman (1975) has pointed out in the context of automobile safety regulations, increasing safety can result in drivers offsetting these gains by taking more risks in how they drive. The same thing is possible with regard to crime. For example, allowing citizens to carry concealed firearms may encourage people to risk entering more dangerous neighborhoods or to begin traveling during times they previously avoided. Thus, since the decision to engage in these riskier activities is a voluntary one, it is possible that society still could be better off even if crime rates were to rise as a result of concealed handgun laws.

Finally, there are also the issues of why certain states adopted concealed handgun laws and whether higher offense rates result in lower arrest rates. To the extent that states adopted the law because crime were rising, ordinary least squares estimates would under predict the drop in crime. Likewise, if the rules were adopted when crimes rates were falling, the bias would be in the opposite direction. None of the previous studies deal with this last type of potential bias. At least since Ehrlich (1973, pp. 548-553), economists have also realized that potential biases exist from having the offense rate as both the endogenous variable and as the denominator in determining the arrest rate and because increasing crime rates may lower the arrest if the same resources are being asked to do more work. Fortunately, both these sets of potential biases can be dealt with using two-stage least-squares.

III. The Data

Between 1977 and 1992, 10 states (Florida (1987), Georgia (1989), Idaho (1990), Maine (1985), Mississippi (1990), Montana (1991), Oregon (1990), Pennsylvania (1989), Virginia (1988), and West Virginia (1989)) adopted "shall issue" right-to-carry firearm laws. However, Pennsylvania is a special case because Philadelphia was exempted from the state law during our sample period. Nine other states (Alabama, Connecticut, Indiana, Maine, New Hampshire, North Dakota, South Dakota, Vermont, and Washington) effectively had these laws on the books prior to the period being studied.[18] Since the data are at the county level, a dummy variable is set equal to one for each county operating under "shall issue" right-to-carry laws. A Nexis search was conducted to determine the exact date on which these laws took effect. For the states that adopted the law during the year, the dummy variable for that year is scaled to equal that portion of the year for which the law was in effect.

While the number of arrests and offenses for each type of crime in every county from 1977 to 1992 were provided by the Uniform Crime Report, we also contacted the state department of corrections, State Attorney Generals, State Secretary of State, and State Police offices in every state to try to compile data on conviction rates, sentence lengths, and right-to-carry concealed weapons permits by county. The Bureau of Justice Statistics also released a list of contacts in every state that might have available state level criminal justice data. Unfortunately, county data on the total number of outstanding right-to-carry pistol permits were available for only Arizona, California, Florida, Oregon, Pennsylvania, and Washington, though time series county data before and after a change in the permitting law was only available for Arizona (1994 to 1996), Oregon (1990 to 1992) and Pennsylvania (1986 to 1992). Since the Oregon "shall issue" law passed in 1990, we attempted to get data on the number of permits in 1989 by calling up every county sheriff in Oregon, with 25 of the 36 counties providing us with this information. (The remaining counties claimed that records had not been kept.)[19] For Oregon, data on the county level conviction rate and prison sentence length was also available from 1977 to 1992.

One difficulty with the sentence length data is that Oregon passed a sentencing reform act that went into effect in November 1989 causing criminals to serve 85 percent of their sentence, and thus judges may have correspondingly altered their rulings. Even then, this change was phased in over time because the law only applied to crimes that took place after it went into effect in 1989. In addition, the Oregon system did not keep complete records prior to 1987, and the completeness of these records decreased the further into the past one went. One solution to both of these problems is to interact the prison sentence length with year dummy variables. A similar problem exists for Arizona which adopted a truth-in-sentencing reform during the fall of 1994. Finally,

Arizona is different from Oregon and Pennsylvania in that it already allowed handguns to be carried openly before passing its concealed handgun law, thus one might expect to find a somewhat smaller response to adopting a concealed handgun law.

In addition to using county dummy variables, other data were collected from the Bureau of the Census to try controlling for other demographic characteristics that might determine the crime rate. These data included information on the population density per square mile, total county population, and detailed information on the racial and age breakdown of the county (percent of population by each racial group and by sex between 10 and 19 years of age, between 20 and 29, between 30 and 39, between 40 and 49, between 50 and 64, and 65 and over). (See Table 2 for the list and summary statistics.) While a large literature discusses the likelihood of younger males engaging in crime (e.g., Wilson and Herrnstein, 1985, pp. 126-147), controlling for these other categories allows us to also attempt to measure the size of the groups considered most vulnerable (e.g., females in the case of rape).[20] Recent evidence by Glaeser and Sacerdote (1995) confirms the higher crime rates experienced in cities and examines to what extent this arises due to social and family influences as well as the changing pecuniary benefits from crime, though this is the first paper to explicitly control for population density. The data appendix provides a more complete discussion of the data.

An additional set of income data was also used. These included real per capita personal income, real per capita unemployment insurance payments, real per capita income maintenance payments, and real per capita retirement payments per person over 65 years of age.[21] Including unemployment insurance and income maintenance payments from the Commerce Department's Regional Economic Information System (REIS) data set were attempts to provide annual county level measures of unemployment and the distribution of income.

Finally, we recognize that other legal changes in penalties involving improper gun use might also have been changing simultaneously with changes in the permitting requirements for concealed handguns. In order to see whether this might confound our ability to infer what was responsible for any observed changes in crimes rates we read through various editions of the Bureau of Alcohol, Tobacco, and Firearms' State Laws and Published Ordinances - Firearms (1976, 1986, 1989, and 1994). Excluding the laws regarding machine guns and sawed-off shotguns, there is no evidence that the laws involving the use of guns changed significantly when concealed permit rules were changed.[22] Another survey which addresses the somewhat boarder question of sentencing enhancement laws for felonies committed with deadly weapons (firearms, explosives, and knives) from 1970-1992 also confirms this general finding with all but four of the legal changes clustered from 1970 to 1981 (Marvell and Moody, 1995, pp. 258-261). Yet, controlling for the dates supplied by Marvell and Moody still allows us to examine the deterrence effect of criminal penalties specifically targeted at the use of deadly weapons during this earlier period.[23]

[...]

VI. Conclusion

Allowing citizens without criminal records or histories of significant mental illness to carry concealed handguns deters violent crimes and appears to produce an extremely small and statistically insignificant change in accidental deaths. If the rest country had adopted right-to-carry concealed handgun provisions in 1992, at least 1,570 murders and over 4,177 rapes would have been avoided. On the other hand, consistent with the notion that criminals respond to incentives, county level data provides evidence that concealed handgun laws are associated with increases in property crimes involving stealth and where the probability of contact between the criminal and the victim are minimal. The largest population counties where the deterrence effect on violent crimes is the greatest is also where the substitution effect into these property crimes is the highest. The estimated annual gain in 1992 from allowing concealed handguns was over $6.21 billion.

The data also supply dramatic evidence supporting the economic notion of deterrence. Higher arrest and conviction rates consistently and dramatically reduce the crime rate. Consistent with other recent work (Kahan, 1996 and Lott, 1992b), the results imply that increasing the arrest rate, independent of the probability of eventual conviction, imposes a significant penalty on criminals. Perhaps the most surprising result is that the deterrence effect of a one percentage point increase in arrest rates is much larger than the same increase in the probability of conviction. Also surprising was that while longer prison lengths usually implied lower crime rates, the results were normally not statistically significant.

This study incorporates a number of improvements over previous studies on deterrence, and it represents a very large change in how gun studies have been done. This is the first study to use cross-sectional time-series evidence for counties at both the national level and for individual states. Instead of simply using cross-sectional state or city level data, our study has made use of the much bigger variations in arrest rates and crime rates between rural and urban areas, and it has been possible to control for whether the lower crime rates resulted from the gun laws themselves or other differences in these areas (e.g., low crime rates) which lead to the adoption of these laws. Equally importantly, our study has allowed us to examine what effect concealed handgun laws have on different counties even within the same state. The evidence indicates that the effect varies both with a county's level of crime and its population.

Bibliography

Andreoni, James, "Criminal Deterrence in the Reduce Form: A New Perspective on Ehrlich's Seminal Study," *Economic Inquiry*, Vol. 33, no. 3 (July 1995): 476-483.

Annest, J.L.; J.A. Mercy; D.R. Gibson; and G.W. Ryan, "National Estimates of NonFatal Firearem-related Injuries, Beyond the Tip of the Iceberg," Journal of the American Medical Association (June 14, 1995): 1749-54.

Barhnhart, Bob, "Concealed Handgun Licensing in Multnomah County," mimeo from the Intelligence/Concealed Handgun Unit: Multnomah County (October 1994).

Block, Michael K. and John Heineke, "A Labor Theoretical Analysis of Criminal Choice," American Economic Review, Vol. 65 (June 1975): 314-325.

Cook, P.J., "The Role of Firearms in Violent Crime," In Wolfgang, M.E. and N.A. Werner (eds.), Criminal Violence, Beverly Hills: Sage Publishers (1982): 236-291.

___, "The Technology of Personal Violence," Crime and Justice: Annual Review of Research, Vol. 14 (1991): 57-87.

___, Stephanie Molliconi, and Thomas B. Cole, "Regulating Gun Markets," Journal of Criminal Law and Criminology, Vol. 86, no. 1 (Fall 1995): 59-92.

Cramer, Clayton E. and David B. Kopel, "Shall Issue': The New Wave of Concealed Handgun Permit Laws," Tennessee Law Review, Vol. 62 (Spring 1995): 679-758, and expanded version of this paper dated 1994 is also available from the Independence Institute, Golden, Colorado.

Ehrlich, Isaac, "Participation in Illegitimate Activities: A Theoretical and Empirical Investigation," Journal of Political Economy, Vol. 81, no. 3 (1973): 521-565.

Federal Bureau of Investigation, Crime in the United States, Federal Bureau of Investigation: Washington, D.C. (editions for 1977 to 1992).

Fort Worth Star-Telegram, "Few Probelms Reported After Allowing Concealed Handguns, Officers Say," Fort Worth Star-Telegram (July 16, 1996).

Glaeser, Edward L. and Bruce Sacerdote, "Why is There More Crime in Cities?" Presented at Symposium in Honor of Gary Becker's 65th Birthday, Harvard University working paper (November 14, 1995).

Greenwald, Bruce C. "A General Analysis of the Bias in the Estimated Standard Errors of Least Squares Coefficients," Journal of Econometrics, Vol. 22 (August 1983): 323-338.

Grossman, Michael, Frank J. Chaloupka, and Charles C. Brown, "The Demand for Cocaine by Young Adults: A Rational Addiction Approach," NBER Working Paper (July 1996).

Japan Economic Newswire, "U.S. jury clears man who shot Japanese student," Kyodo News Service (May 24, 1993).

Kahan, Dan M., "What Do Alternative Sanctions Mean?," University of Chicago Law Review, Vol. 63, no. 1 (1996): 591-653.

Kleck, Gary, "Guns and Violence: An Interpretive Review of the Field," Social Pathology, Vol. 1, no. 1 (January 1995): 12-47.

____ and E. Britt Patterson, "The Impact of Gun Control and Gun Ownership Levels on Violence Rates," Journal of Quantitative Criminology, Vol. 9 (1993): 249-287.

____ and Marc Gertz, "Armed Resistance to Crime: The Prevalence and Nature of Self-Defense with a Gun," Journal of Criminal Law and Criminology, Vol. 86, no. 1 (Fall 1995): 150-187.

Kopel, David B., The Samuri, the Mountie, and the Cowboy, Prometheus Books: Buffalo, New York (1992).

____, Guns: Who Should Have Them?, Prometheus Books: Buffalo, New York (1995).

Landes, William M., "An Economic Study of U.S. Aircraft Hijacking, 1961-1976," Journal of Law and Economics, Vol. 21, no. 1 (April 1978): 1-31.

Levitt, Steven, "The Effect of Prison Population Size on Crime Rates: Evidence from Prison Overcrowding Litigation," Quarterly Journal of Economics (1996).

Lipton, Eric, "Virginians Get Ready to Conceal Arms; State's New Weapon Law Brings a Flood of Inquiries," The Washington Post (June 28, 1995): A1.

Lott, John R., Jr., "Juvenile Delinquency and Education: A Comparison of Public and Private Provision," International Review of Law and Economics, Vol.7, no. 2 (December 1987): 163-175.

____, "A Transaction-Costs Explanation for Why the Poor are More Likely to Commit Crime," Journal of Legal Studies, Vol. 19, no. 1 (January 1990a): 243-245.

___, "The Effect of Conviction on the Legitimate Income of Criminals," Economics Letters, Vol. 34, no. 12 (December 1990b): 381-385.

___, "An Attempt at Measuring the Total Monetary Penalty from Drug Convictions: The Importance of an Individual's Reputation," Journal of Legal Studies, Vol. 21, no. 1 (January 1992a): 159-187.

___, "Do We Punish High Income Criminals too Heavily?" Economic Inquiry, Vol. 30, no. 4 (October 1992b): 583-608.

___, "Now That The Brady Law is Law, You Are Not Any Safer Than Before," Philadelphia Inquirer, Tuesday, February 1, 1994, p. A9.

Marvell, Thomas B. and Carlisle E. Moody, "The Impact of Enhanced Prison Terms for Felonies Committed with Guns," Criminology, Vol. 33, no. 2 (May 1995): 247-282.

McCormick, Robert E. and Robert Tollison, "Crime on the Court," Journal of Political Economy, Vol. 92, no. 2 (April 1984): 223-235.

McDowall, David; Colin Loftin; and Brian Wiersema, "Easing Conealed Firearm Laws: Effects on Homicide in Three States," Journal of Criminal Law and Criminology, Vol. 86, no. 1 (Fall 1995): 193-206.

Miller, Ted R.; Mark A. Cohen; and Brian Wiersema, Victim Costs and Consequences: A New Look, National Institute of Justice: Washington, D.C. (February 1996).

Moulton, Brent R., "An Illusration of a Pitfall in Estimating the Effects of Aggregate Variables on Micro Units," Review of Economics and Statistics, Vol. 72 (1990): 334-338.

Peltzman, Sam, "The Effects of Automobile Safety Regulation," Journal of Political Economy Vol. 883, no. 4 (August 1975): 677-725.

Polsby, Daniel D., "Firearms Costs, Firearms Benefits and the Limits of Knowledge," Journal of Criminal Law and Criminology, Vol. 86, no. 1 (Fall 1995): 207-220.

Potok, Mark, "Texan says gun law saved his life'I did what I thought I had to do," USA TODAY (March 22, 1996): 3A.

Rasmusen, Eric, "Stigma and Self-Fulfilling Expectations of Criminality," Journal of Law and Economics, forthcoming October 1996.

Reynolds, Morgan O., "Crime and Punishment in America," National Center for Policy Analysis, Policy Report 193 (June 1995).

Sharn, Lori, "Violence shoots holes in USA's tourist image," USA TODAY (September 9, 1993): 2A.

Southwick, Lawrence, Jr., "Self-defense with Guns: The Consequences," SUNY Buffalo working paper (1996).

Uviller, H. Richard, Virtual Justice, Yale University Press: New Haven (1996).

Will, George F., "Are We 'a Nation of Cowards'?" Newsweek (November 15, 1993): 93-94.

Zimring, Franklin, "Is Gun Control Likely to Reduce Violent Killings?," University of Chicago Law Review, Vol. 35 (1968).

____, "The Medium is the Message: Firearm Caliber as a Determinant of Death from Assult" Journal of Legal Studies, Vol. 1 (1972): 97-123.

____, "Firearms and Federal Law: The Gun Control Act of 1968" Journal of Legal Studies, Vol. 4 (1975): 133-198.

5

Guns Will Change the Character of Higher Education

Steven J. Friesen

Steven J. Friesen is the Louise Farmer Boyer Chair in Biblical Studies at the University of Texas at Austin. His research focus is early Christianity, with particular interests in the book of Revelation, poverty in the Roman Empire, and archaeology of religion in the eastern Mediterranean.

In 2015, Texas passed Senate Bill II, which expanded the scope of open carry on the state's public university campuses. This law became effective on August 1, 2016. While Texas is not the only state to allow open carry on its campuses, the decision was based on a strong culture that may be unique to the Lone Star State. While many educators view individual thought and critical thinking skills as some of the hallmarks of higher education, the Texas government believes that obedience to authority is much more important. The presence of firearms in university classrooms, which many argue should be "safe spaces," is a direct extension of that ideology, and it immediately upsets the balance and the mission of higher learning.

As of Aug. 1, 2016, a new law allows concealed handguns in college and university buildings in Texas.

It's already had an impact on me as professor of religious studies at the University of Texas at Austin. Thanks to this law, I set foot in a federal court building for the first time.

And I was not alone. The courtroom was packed. Other citizens were there as well to support three professors who are suing the state's attorney general and the University of Texas for the right to ban guns from their own classrooms.

Why are these professors taking the extraordinary step of suing the state of Texas and their own university?

In order to understand the situation, we need to consider the political tensions between the legislature and the university, the ideological struggle over the goals of higher education and the possible dangers of bringing more guns to campuses.

Campus carry law in Texas

Until this year, Texas law allowed anyone with a Concealed Handgun License (CHL) to carry a loaded hidden gun on campus, but not inside buildings. This restriction kept down the number of people carrying weapons legally on campus.

During the 2015 legislative session, a majority of Republicans pushed the idea to allow guns on campus. University administrators, faculty, faculty council, staff, undergraduate and graduate students and campus police overwhelmingly opposed the idea.

However, in spite of campus opposition, in May 2015, the proposed law, known as Senate Bill 11 (SB 11), was approved. So, as of Aug. 1, 2016, anyone with a concealed handgun license can carry a loaded, semiautomatic pistol into most offices, classrooms, hallways, public spaces, cafeterias and gyms at state universities. All that they need: four hours of training and a score of 70 percent accuracy on a shooting test.

Supporters argue that Americans have a constitutional right to protect themselves and carry weapons with as few limits as possible. Carrying guns into classrooms, they say, is part of that right.

Clash of ideologies

For many of us, however, this conflict is about a larger ideological battle over the goals and character of higher education in Texas, with one side emphasizing obedience to authority and the other the need to critique authority.

Let's consider these two views of education.

The ideology of higher education in the U.S. has historically focused on critical thinking, and faculty overwhelmingly see this as the primary goal (see especially Table 3) of college and university classes. According to this view, universities and colleges are encouraged to question orthodoxy. In other words, higher education should subject all truth claims to intense scrutiny.

The goal of this process is not to tear down society but to make it better, to allow us to develop our full potential as individuals and as a nation in the pursuit of liberty and justice.

But here is where the conflict comes in. As the discussion below shows, the campus carry movement has, it seems, a different ideology for higher education. The underlying motivation is that traditional authority must be maintained and, in the end, disagreement is resolved by force, not by debate. For this ideology, critical thinking is a potential threat to authority.

Republican Party principles

Evidence for this comes from the ideas expressed in the Texas Republican Party platform, a formal declaration of the principles on which a party stands and makes it appeal to voters.

The 2012 Texas Republican Party Platform took an explicit stand against "critical thinking skills and similar programs…that focus on behavior modification and have the purpose of challenging the student's fixed beliefs and undermining parental authority."

Subsequently, the 2016 Texas Republican Platform stepped back from that extreme statement. But it still asserted that parents or guardians – not the government – should have ultimate control over the education of their children.

In the 2016 platform, both guns and religion are discussed in the section on education. Here is what it looks like:

The section on education supports the radical position that all law-abiding citizens should be able to carry guns anywhere without restriction. It says,

> "We collectively urge the legislature to pass 'constitutional carry' legislation, whereby law-abiding citizens that possess firearms can legally exercise their God-given right to carry that firearm as well. We call for the elimination of all gun free zones. All federal acts, laws, executive orders, and court orders which restrict or infringe on the people's right to keep and bear arms shall be invalid in Texas, not be recognized by Texas, shall be specifically rejected by Texas, and shall be considered null and void and of no effect in Texas."

Another paragraph in the education section discusses "safeguarding religious liberties." This one begins by saying,

> "We affirm that the public acknowledgment of God is undeniable in our history and is vital to our freedom, prosperity, and strength."

It goes on to denounce "the myth of separation of church and state," and it supports the right of businesses to refuse service to anyone based on religious conviction.

What this does is to reaffirm the ideology of the Republican Party of Texas – that education should be governed by traditional authorities of family and conservative forms of Protestant Christianity and not by critical inquiry.

In other words, religious commitment of individuals is more important than civil rights. Furthermore, according to this traditionalist view of authority, liberty and safety are preserved not so much by critique and analysis as by encouraging everyone to carry a gun.

Views from ground zero

This raises the question of how this ideology affects students and professors in the classroom.

As the political battle raged in the Texas legislature in spring 2016, I taught a science and religion class in which we spent the semester analyzing the volatile debates in the U.S. about human evolution and creationism.

I asked my students how they would feel about the possible presence of guns in classrooms.

One student self-identified as having a concealed handgun license and did not have trouble with the presence of guns. But most others thought that it would make them more cautious and less forthright in class. One student said she would be vigilant about how other students were acting. Another said she would censor her opinions.

The sentiment they expressed was confirmed in anonymous polling I conducted before our discussion. Two students (11 percent) were in favor of concealed carry on campus as demanded by SB 11, while 13 (68 percent) thought guns should be completely illegal on campus except for law officers. Only three students (16 percent) felt that SB 11 would make them safer, while 11 (58 percent) expected that the law would make campus less safe.

While one class is hardly a representative sample, these numbers reflect discussions I've had with my classes over the last few semesters. The numbers also match a variety of conversations I've had on campus.

What might change on campus?

As a professor, I have other concerns for my students beyond the classroom. We work with students at a difficult time in their lives as they work through the transition to adulthood. Some of them also face serious emotional issues. When I have to deal with failed exams, missed assignments and occasional plagiarism or cheating, I sometimes worry about how they will respond.

So far I have not encountered physical threats to my own safety, but I know faculty who have. While waiting in line for the security screening at the federal courthouse, I learned of two more examples. One was a professor of computer sciences who told me about the time when he was physically shoved and verbally abused by a student who got a B rather than an A.

He decided not to press charges. But when the legislature passed the campus carry law, he retired rather than face the possibility of legal weapons in university buildings. Another faculty member told of the time she had to convince her dean to drop a student from her class mid-semester for anti-Semitic remarks the student made about her.

Systematic studies point toward other problems that await us if we increase the number of guns on campus. We can expect more accidental shootings, more successful suicide attempts and perhaps even an increase in sexual assaults. In the event of an actual active shooter event, we can expect that an armed civilian will make no difference or even make the situation worse.

Will guns change the character of higher education?

The ideological struggle will continue. Polling early in 2015 showed that Texans were divided on campus carry: 47 percent were in favor, 45 percent were opposed and 8 percent were unsure (this included 22 percent strongly supporting and 32 percent strongly opposed). Campus protests and a satirical student campaign against SB 11 are planned.

Supporters of the law have filed a formal complaint with the attorney general's office to make the law stronger by preventing faculty and staff from banning guns in their own offices. Legal papers filed by the University of Texas and the state attorney general have stated that professors would face disciplinary measures if they barred guns from classrooms. There is significant political pressure and special interest money to expand gun rights.

If the lawsuit of the three professors is not successful, we will begin to find out fairly soon what difference SB 11 will actually make in real lives – in the classroom, in the relationships of students, faculty and staff – and in the character of higher education in an American setting.

The actual difference will not be abstract or theoretical. Both opponents and supporters of SB 11 claim that the struggle over guns on campus is a matter of life and death.

6

Firearm Self Defense Legality

Lauren Baldwin

Lauren Baldwin has been licensed as an attorney in New Mexico for twenty years. She holds a Juris Doctor from the University of New Mexico School of Law.

What constitutes the legitimate use of a licensed firearm for self-defense? Prior to using a gun, a victim must first make an attempt to retreat from an assailant. If this is impossible, another stipulation is that force should be proportional. The use of deadly force on an unarmed attacker would complicate a claim of self-defense. The exception to this rule is in the home, where one is legally entitled to defend one's "castle". In several states, controversial "Stand Your Ground" laws expand this doctrine outside the home. In Florida, the killing of unarmed teenager Trayvon Martin was unjustly claimed as self-defense under such a law.

A person is entitled to use a gun for self defense in the U.S., if necessary, but laws in every state establish when a person can use force to defend himself (or another), and whether a person can use a weapon. Someone who intends to carry or keep a gun for self defense purposes should follow state laws on gun ownership and carrying concealed weapons. (You can learn the laws in your state regarding gun permits and open and concealed carry laws by starting with Gun Possession and Use Laws and Concealed Weapon Laws.)

"Using a Gun for Self Defense: Laws and Consequences," by Lauren Baldwin, Nolo.com. Reprinted by permission.

Laws Governing Gun Ownership and Use

All states have laws requiring that guns be registered, as well as laws prohibiting certain people, such as convicted felons, from owning guns. Some states outlaw certain firearms such as some types of automatic rifles or firearms with silencers. If you intend to carry a firearm or keep a gun in your home for protection, you should choose only a weapon that is legal in your state. If you intend to carry a concealed firearm—in your purse or inside a jacket and not in plain view—you should check on whether your state permits "concealed carry" and what permit or license you need.

While using an illegal weapon or not having a concealed carry permit will not prevent you from claiming self defense, it could cast you in a suspicious light with law enforcement or complicate an already potentially complicated case if you have to use the weapon in self defense.

Traditional Self Defense

The law governing self defense does not excuse any violent act just because another person struck the first blow or made a violent threat. Traditional self defense laws require a person who is being attacked or threatened with imminent attack to act reasonably and

- retreat if possible without taking any physical action, and
- use only the amount of force reasonably necessary to fend off the attacker.

Retreat if possible

If an able-bodied man raises a fist or hits another able-bodied man, under traditional self defense laws the victim must walk away if possible. If the victim is charged with a crime and claims self defense, the jury must consider whether the victim had a reasonable opportunity to retreat and did not take it. If the victim could easily have left the room or walked away from the offender, the victim's use of physical force might not constitute self defense. To support a successful self-defense argument, the evidence must show that the victim could not retreat—for example, that he could not get away because the attack was ongoing, he was trapped with the aggressor behind a locked door, the aggressor blocked the exit, or the victim tried to leave or walk away and the aggressor followed him.

Reasonable force

If the victim could not retreat, the jury usually next must consider whether the victim was reasonably in fear for his physical safety and whether any force the victim used was reasonable. The test is often whether a reasonable person in similar circumstances would be afraid and would act as the defendant did.

Under traditional self defense laws, the act of brandishing or using a gun is evaluated like any other use of force. The primary question is whether using a gun was reasonable or reasonably necessary under the circumstances. A victim cannot instantly pull a gun and shoot an attacker who raises a fist or slaps or punches the victim without trying to fend him off in some other way, because this amounts to using more force than was reasonably necessary to stop the attack. If a person uses deadly force to fend off an attack, he must have been in fear that he was about to be gravely injured or killed. The victim also must have had a reasonable basis for fearing for his life, such as dealing with an aggressor who was pointing a gun, wielding another deadly weapon, or acting in a way that could cause death or serious bodily harm.

What if the aggressor doesn't have a gun?

The facts of the situation are always very important when it comes to questions of self defense. If an attacker waives or shoots a gun, pulling a gun or shooting back usually will constitute self defense. In some situations, using a gun in self defense also may be appropriate even if the aggressor does not have a gun. For instance, if an attacker has another deadly weapon such as a knife, a metal bar or a baseball bat, using a gun can be considered reasonable if the victim can't access any other weapon.

A victim also might be justified in showing a weapon and warning that he will shoot if necessary, even if the aggressor has no weapon and is threatening or attacking the victim with his fists or other parts of body. If the victim who brandished the gun is charged with threatening another person with a deadly weapon, he can present evidence that he showed the gun in self defense—to get the assailant to back off.

The "Castle Doctrine"

In general, people who are under attack in their own homes don't need to retreat or try to escape, even if they can do so safely. Instead, they can typically "stand their ground" and use force—even enough force to kill—if they are in apparent danger of serious injury. The theory is that people shouldn't have to run within or from their own homes—that they should be free to defend their "castles."

"Stand Your Ground"

As many as 32 states recently have adopted "stand your ground" laws that expand traditional self defense laws and extend the castle doctrine to confrontations outside a person's home. (For more information on the stand your ground defense, see "Stand Your Ground" *New Trends in Self-Defense Law*.)

The stand your ground defense may apply and permit a victim to brandish or use a firearm, depending on state law, in the following situations:

- Beyond the house. If a person is confronted in his vehicle or on his residential property including the driveway, swimming pool area, or land around the home, he may respond with a firearm.
- A public place. If an aggressor uses force or threatens violence against another in a public place, the person being attacked or threatened has no duty to choose an apparent safe way to retreat, and may instead use the amount of reasonable force necessary to fend off the attacker.

Consult an Attorney

If you are charged with a crime, you should contact an attorney who is familiar with the criminal law in your state. If you used a gun in self defense, you also should contact an attorney whether or not you have been charged with a crime. An experienced attorney can advise you of the law regarding guns and self defense and represent you in a criminal case, if necessary.

7

Concealed Carry Prevents Shootings

Crime Prevention Research Center

The Crime Prevention Research Center is a research and education organization that conducts academic quality research on gun laws and their relationship to crime and safety.

In Chicago, an Uber driver prevented a possible mass shooting by shooting and wounding a man who was firing into a crowd. The driver had a permit to legally carry a concealed weapon and claimed to be acting in self-defense and the defense of others, thus no charges were filed against him. In the following excerpt, The Crime Prevention Research Center examines a few similar cases in which concealed carry laws have possibly prevented more deadly shooting events. The plausible conclusion is that concealed carry laws make us safer, however, opponents of concealed carry might justly question whether these cases are indeed the norm or exceptional outliers.

This past Friday, an Uber driver with a permitted concealed handgun stopped what likely would have been a mass public shooting. Police arrived on the scene quickly, but the Uber driver had still already taken care of the situation before they arrived. From Mitch Dudek in the *Chicago Sun-Times* (April 2015):

> An Uber driver put his concealed carry permit to use Friday night when he pulled a gun and opened fire on a man he saw

"Updated: Compiling Cases Where Concealed Handgun Permit Holders Have Stopped Mass Public Shootings and Other Mass Attacks," Crime Prevention Research Center, September 20, 2016. Reprinted by permission.

firing a pistol into a group of people on a Logan Square sidewalk, according to prosecutors.

Six blasts from his gun injured a 22-year-old man identified as Everardo Custodio.

Custodio suffered wounds to his shin, knee and lower back . . . Cook County Judge Peggy Chiampas refused to grant [Custodio] bail on charges of aggravated battery with a firearm and illegal possession of a firearm.

The 47-year-old Uber driver "was acting in self-defense and in the defense of others," Assistant State's Attorney Barry Quinn said. . . .

The Uber driver had dropped off a passenger minutes before the shooting occurred, said Uber spokeswoman Jen Mullin. She had no comment on the driver's actions other than to say the company requires all its drivers to abide by local, state and federal laws pertaining to transporting firearms in vehicles. . . .

Police patrolling the area heard the shots and arrived to find Custodio on the ground and bleeding. Police also recovered a handgun found near Custodio, Quinn said. . . .

[The Uber driver is] a registered gun owner who has a concealed carry license. He doesn't face any charges. . . .

In a *Washington Post* column, Eugene Volokh asks: "Have civilians with permitted concealed handguns stopped such mass shootings before?" We provided Volokh with a list of cases that used.

The Uber driver case isn't even the first mass public shooting in Chicago that has been stopped by a concealed handgun permit holder.

Chicago, July 7, 2014, from Geoff Ziezulewicz in the *Chicago Tribune:*

A Gresham man fired on a group of people leaving a party, only to be shot himself by one of the victims, a military service member with a concealed carry permit, authorities said.

The military member and three others were leaving a party Friday night . . .

One of the victims had noticed a cup of liquor on top of her vehicle and asked attendees of a party next door who it belonged to, Hain said.

When she removed it, Denzel A. Mickiel approached her, shouting obscenities and threatening her and her friends, according to Hain and court records. . . .

As Mickiel fired at the victims' vehicle, the military member retrieved his gun and took cover near the vehicle's front fender, according to Hain. Two unidentified people also shot at the group, she said.

The military service member fired two shots and struck Mickiel twice, she said.

A 22-year-old woman in the group was injured by Mickiel in the shooting, suffering wounds to the arm and back, according to court records and Hain.

The four victims escaped the melee in two vehicles as two unidentified people continued to shoot at them, Hain said. . . .

A note: A concern is often raise that a concealed handgun permit holder who stops an attack might accidentally shoot a bystander or might himself be accidentally shot by the police. In none of these cases has that occurred. As noted below, it is very likely that we do not have all the cases where a permit holder stops a mass public shooting, but if a permit holder were to shoot a bystander, it seems clear that such a case would get news coverage. Thus it seems pretty certain that such cases don't occur during these types of events.

Some other cases include

Note that most all these cases have just a couple of local news stories on them. There is no reason to believe that this list is comprehensive given how little media coverage is given to mass public shootings that were stopped by concealed handgun permit holders. Even in the cases that got massive news coverage, only a few of those stories would mention that it was a permit holder who stopped the attack. In addition, there is no attempt here to list here the very large number of defensive gun uses that are reported daily in the US. This list here only includes cases where mass public shootings were stopped.

Lyman, South Carolina, June 30, 2016 (Fox Carolina)

Just a couple of weeks after the Orlando massacre, man, 32-year-old Jody Ray Thompson, started shooting at others at another nightclub. Fortunately, unlike Florida, permitted concealed handguns were allowed in bars in South Carolina. Before he could shoot a fourth person, the permit holder was able shoot back, wounding Thompson in the leg.

> "His rounds struck 3 victims, and almost struck a fourth victim, who in self-defense, pulled his own weapon and fired, striking Thompson in the leg," Lt. Kevin Bobo said.
>
> Bobo said the man who shot Thompson has a valid concealed weapons permit, cooperated with investigators, and won't be facing any charges. . . . .

> Also this

> and at least one South Carolina sheriff [is] crediting a man with a concealed carry permit with preventing further violence at a nightclub . . .

Winton, Ohio, Sunday, July 26, 2015, Fox 19 in Cincinnati and Fox News

The shooter in this case directly fired at four different people. Fortunately, because of the permit holder's quick actions, no one was seriously injured.

> [Thomas] McCary [62-years-old] was arguing with a woman around 8 p.m. Sunday night and, when the woman's brother, Patrick Ewing, approached, McCary pulled out a .38-caliber handgun and fired three shots at him, Cincinnati police said.
>
> Ewing didn't get hit, but he did get his own gun and returned fire, wounding McCary in the leg. Ewing had a permit to carry a concealed weapon.
>
> Injured, McCary went into his house to get a second gun and, holding a weapon in each hand, he fired three shots in the direction of the woman, Jeaneta Walker, her 1-year-old son and a third man.

Ewing fired at McCary again to try to distract him as the victims fled indoors. McCary squeezed off a few more rounds, hitting no one, before withdrawing into his apartment, Cincinnati.com reported. . . .

Conyers, Georgia, Sunday, May 31, 2015, *The Rockdale Citizen*
Often it is claimed that citizens who stop mass public shootings don't get news coverage because they stop anyone from being killed. But in this case two people were killed before the permit holder was able to stop the attack.

A customer who fired back at the suspect who killed two people in a Ga. Highway 20 liquor store Sunday afternoon is being hailed as a hero.

Rockdale County Sheriff Eric Levett said at a press conference Monday that Todd C. Scott, 44, a resident of Covington, very likely prevented other customers in the store from losing their lives.

Levett said store video from Magnet Bottle Shop showed that the suspect, Jeffrey Scott Pitts, 36, came in the store Sunday afternoon firing a handgun.

"I believe that if Mr. Scott did not return fire at the suspect then more of those customers would have hit by a gun," said [Rockdale County Sheriff Eric Levett]. "It didn't appear that he cared who he shot or where he was shooting until someone was shooting back at him. So in my opinion he saved other lives in that store."

From the *Atlanta Journal Constitution*:

Pitts fled after another patron, Todd C. Scott, of Covington, opened fire with his own hand gun. It is still unclear whether Aikens died before or after Scott returned fire with Pitts, but the sheriff credited Scott with saving lives.

"I consider him to be a hero," [Rockdale County Sheriff Eric Levett] said.

New Holland, South Carolina, May 5th, 2015, Fox Carolina (cases such as this where the people who stopped the attack didn't fire a gun don't tend to get that much news attention):

The Aiken County Sheriff's Office said deputies responded to the New Holland Fire Department's Station 2 around 6:30 p.m. for a report of shots fired.

Firefighters said Chad Barker pulled up to the crowded fire station parking lot full of children and firefighters, got out of his car, and began firing in the air and at his vehicle. They say he also pointed the firearm at individual firefighters for lengthy periods of time.

"I came out of the office, saw the man with the gun, told everybody to leave out the back quickly that there was a man in the parking lot with a gun, and I was not kidding," said Gary Knoll, a firefighter for New Holland.

Knoll said he and another firefighter who have concealed weapons permits pulled their guns on the gunman.

Knoll said Barker returned to his vehicle and firefighters carefully followed him with their weapons still drawn. After encouraging Barker to put the gun down, Knoll said Barker ultimately complied and Knoll grabbed the gun. . . .

Philadelphia, Pennsylvania, March 2015, NBC Channel 10: Police say a man likely saved the lives of several people when he shot and killed a gunman inside a West Philadelphia barbershop.

A 40-year-old man was inside Falah Barber Shop Inc. on the 600 block of Preston Street shortly before 3 p.m. Sunday when police say he began fighting with another person inside. . . .

The fight quickly escalated and the 40-year-old man took out his gun and opened fire on customers and barbers, police said. , , ,

As he was shooting, another man outside heard the gunfire, ran into the shop and took out his own gun, according to investigators. He then opened fire, striking the 40-year-old man once in the chest. . . .

"The person who responded was a legal gun permit carrier," said Philadelphia Police Captain Frank Llewellyn. "He responded and I guess he saved a lot of people in there."

Darby, Pennsylvania, July 2014, John Lott in the *Philadelphia Inquirer* (Other details on the case are available here).

The attacker, Richard Plotts, is a convicted felon, which bans him from legally owning a gun. . . .

At Mercy Fitzgerald, caseworker Theresa Hunt was killed when Plotts opened fire during a regularly scheduled appointment with Dr. Lee Silverman. Fortunately, the doctor had his own gun and returned fire, hitting Plotts three times and critically wounding him.

After firing all the bullets in his gun, Plotts still had 39 bullets on him, bullets that he could have used to shoot many other people . . .

Portland, Oregon, January 11, 2014, *Oregonian*

Thomas Eliot Hjelmeland, 43-years-old, was ejected from a night club, but he returned 30 minutes later with a gun and wearing a mask. He shot the bouncer who had ejected him and shot at others. The bouncer was shot in the head and critically wounded. Two others were also wounded: one patron in the foot and a waitress, who had been standing at the front of the club, in both of her legs. Hjelmeland was on probation at the time of the incident. Given that Hjelmeland was shooting people all around the club, Bouncer Jonathan Baer, a concealed handgun permit holder who fatally shot Hjelmeland, appears to have had good reason to fear that other people at the front of the club would also have been shot by Hjelmeland.

Here is a February 1, 2014 article in the *Oregonian*.

Baer, 31, followed the masked gunman out of the club's interior doors to the entrance foyer and drew his own Glock .40-caliber pistol from his hip. He looked back one or two times to check on Rizzo, who hadn't gotten up.

While using one foot to prop open the club's inner door, Baer said he saw the masked man reach the front door. The man stopped and looked as if he were going to turn around. Baer said he leaned forward and fired two to three rounds.

Baer, who has a concealed handgun license, . . .

Baer later explained to detectives that he had thought about two dancers and two customers who were standing outside the club smoking. He said he didn't want anyone else to get hurt. . . .

And this January 21, 2014 article in the *Oregonian*.

Club co-owner Connie Barnes said she did not know Baer was armed that night, but she called him a hero.

In a Facebook post, Baer wrote, "I did what I felt was right to stop the shooter…I carry every day, and will continue to, and will so with the hope that I will NEVER have to pull it out again." . . .

Portland, Oregon, December 2012 KGW Staff:

Meli is emotionally drained. The 22-year-old was at Clackamas Town Center with a friend and her baby when a masked man opened fire.

"I heard three shots and turned and looked at Casey and said, 'are you serious?,'" he said.

The friend and baby hit the floor. Meli, who has a concealed carry permit, positioned himself behind a pillar.

He was working on his rifle, said Meli. He kept pulling the charging handle and hitting the side.

The break in gunfire allowed Meli to pull out his own gun, but he never took his eyes off the shooter.

"As I was going down to pull, Isaw someone in the back of the Charlotte move, and Iknew if Ifired and missed, I could hit them," he said.. . .

I'm not beating myself up cause I didn't shoot him, said Meli. Iknow after he saw me, I think the last shot he fired was the one he used on himself. . . .

Plymouth, Pennsylvania, September 2012, article by Bob Kalinowski Citizensvoice.com

. . . It's the gun prosecutors said Ktytor used to put an end to a 26-year-old man's shooting rampage on Sept. 9, 2012 in Plymouth.

Ever since Ktytor, who has a concealed carry license, dropped the killer with several shots on Main Street in Plymouth, . . .

In October, the murder suspect, William Allabaugh of Plymouth, pleaded guilty to third-degree murder and attempted murder, then was sentenced to 25 to 50 years in state prison.

Authorities say Allabaugh critically wounded Stephen Hollman, 30, by shooting him in the head inside Bonnie's Food and Spirits on Main Street. A short time later, Allabaugh fatally shot Scott Luzetsky, 39, outside the bar. Police said both victims were innocent bystanders who didn't provoke the attack by Allabaugh, who was angered he was being kicked out of the bar.

More importantly see this (emphasis added):

"The video footage and the evidence reveals that Mr. Allabaugh had turned around and was reapproaching the bar. Mr. [Ktytor] then acted, taking him down. We believe that it could have been much worse that night," Luzerne County A.D.A. Jarrett Ferentino said.

Early, Texas, August, 2012, KTXS ABC Channel 12:

An armed citizen, Vic Stacy, shot and stopped a deranged man who had just murdered two neighbors and was firing at police with a rifle. Stacy made a very long shot with his revolver, three times as far as the perpetrator was from the police officer, who had an AR-15 type rifle.

Santa Clara, California, July 26, 2012, *Reuters*:

. . . 21-year-old Richard Gable Stevens, was subdued after tense moments Monday evening at a shooting range and gun store in this town 30 miles (48 km) south of San Francisco.

"He intended to go out in a blaze of glory," Morec said, noting Stevens had accumulated more than 100 rounds of ammunition for his rented 9mm semi-automatic weapon.

"It certainly looks like he intended to take a lot more people out." . . . .

After several minutes on the range, however, Stevens returned to the club's gun store and shot at the ceiling. He then herded three store employees out the door into an alley, saying he intended to kill them, Morec said.

Unknown to Stevens, one store employee was carrying a .45 caliber handgun concealed beneath his shirt. When Stevens looked away, the employee fired, hitting Stevens several times in the chest and bringing him to the ground. . . . .

Salt Lake, April 27, 2012, ABC Channel 4, Original story is no longer available, but this is its content:

A citizen with a gun stopped a knife wielding man as he began stabbing people Thursday evening at the downtown Salt Lake City Smith's store. Police say the suspect purchased a knife inside the store and then turned it into a weapon. Smith's employee Dorothy Espinoza says, "He pulled it out and stood outside the Smiths in the foyer. And just started stabbing people and yelling you killed my people. You killed my people." Espinoza says, the knife wielding man seriously injured two people. "There is blood all over. One got stabbed in the stomach and got stabbed in the head and held his hands and got stabbed all over the arms." Then, before the suspect could find another victim – a citizen with a gun stopped the madness. "A guy pulled gun on him and told him to drop his weapon or he would shoot him. So, he dropped his weapon and the people from Smith's grabbed him." . . .

Another media report is available here: Lt. Brian Purvis noted "This was a very volatile situation that could have gotten even worse. We can only assume, judging from what we saw, that it could have gotten a lot worse so he [the permit holder] was definitely in the right place at the right time." A brief description is available here.

Aurora, Colorado, April 2012, Fox 31 Denver by Tammy Vigil:

Kiarron Parker rammed his car into another in the church parking lot, got out and attempted to kill multiple church members. He was only able to kill one before a member of the congregation, the nephew of the lady killed, and an off duty police officer, drew his handgun and shot Parker, stopping the killing.

Spartanburg, South Carolina, March 2012, article by Jenny Arnold at GoUpState.com (see also here):

. . . About 11:20 a.m., Jesse Gates returned to the church. The Rev. Guyton's grandson, Aaron Guyton, 26, was in the recreation building separate from the church and saw Gates get a shotgun from the trunk of his car.

"At that point, I knew I had to do something," Aaron Guyton said. "I wanted to try to contain him outside."

Aaron Guyton went into the main building and locked the doors.

Henry Guyton said he was in the pulpit, preaching about how Jesus spoke the word of God and healed the sick, when Gates kicked open the side door of the sanctuary and entered with the shotgun, pointing it at the pastor and congregation.

Church members, including Aaron Guyton, a concealed weapons permit holder, acted quickly.

Aaron Guyton held Gates at gunpoint, as church members Jesse Smith and Leland Powers held him on the floor and waited for deputies to arrive. The Rev. Guyton said he stepped onto a chair, climbed down a 3-foot bannister surrounding the pulpit and took the shotgun from Jesse Gates. . . .

No shots were fired and no one was injured, according to deputies.

During a news conference Sunday, Wright called Aaron and Henry Guyton, Jesse Smith and Leland Powers "everyday heroes." . . .

Oklahoma City, December 2009, KWTV NEWS Channel 9:

. . . Police said the man started firing multiple shots in the parking lot of the Tammaron Village apartments around 4 p.m. Thursday.

Witnesses said the man initially went into the apartment complex's main office. When employees locked him out, he opened fire in the parking lot.

As the man was firing shots, another citizen armed with a gun came around the corner and ordered the gunman to put his weapon down. The gunman dropped his weapon and ran into his father's apartment and barricaded himself inside. . . .

Richmond, Virginia, July 2009 (this first description is based on a video of the shooting and an talk on the attack is here):

The gun owner was in the store [the Golden Market] waiting in line to pay for an item when the bad guy came in wearing dark sunglasses and trying to coverup his face while brandishing a revolver. The [bad guy] yelled for everyone to get down and before anybody could react, immediately walked over to the store owner and in a cold-blooded fashion shot him twice. The owner then dropped down behind the counter. . . .

The [bad guy] ran towards the back of the store, aiming his gun at an innocent man laying prone on the floor. Luckily the [bad guy] was too distracted by the [gun owner] to shoot the man. There is no doubt in my mind that the man would have been shot in cold blood that day if it weren't for that [gun owner] returning fire. . . .

As he approached the front of one aisle, he again pointed a gun at a person on the ground and was about to execute him, when he was again distracted by the [gun owner]. . . .

[…]

8

Should Applicants Provide Reasons for Wanting a Concealed Weapon?

Joseph Blocher

Joseph Blocher is Professor of Law at Duke University. His principal academic interests include federal and state constitutional law, the First and Second Amendments, capital punishment, and property.

The Second Amendment guarantees the right to bear arms within the bounds of one's private property, but should this right extend to public spaces unrestricted? This may be the most important issue in contemporary gun policy. Presently, states can either adopt a "shall issue" or "may issue" stance with regard to concealed carry permits. Populous "may issue" states such as New York and California require applicants to have a compelling reason to carry a gun in public. The difficulty lies in determining the difference between perceived and actual self-defense needs. Thus, some states believe that the right to bear arms does not require a reason.

Can the government require a person to give reasons before lawfully carrying a gun in public? If so, what reasons must it accept?

The answers to these questions remain somewhat unclear, but their importance is difficult to overstate. Licensing requirements for public carrying — especially concealed carrying — are central

Reprinted with permission of Harvard Law Review, from "Good Cause Requirements for Carrying Guns in Public," by Joseph Blocher, Harvard Law Review, Vol. 127 (6), April 11, 2014. Permission conveyed through Copyright Clearance Center, Inc.

to the regulation of guns in public spaces, which is perhaps the most important issue in contemporary gun law and policy. As a constitutional matter, that issue is the crux of recent cases that have found or assumed a right to carry guns in public for self-defense. As a statutory matter, some states have expanded the right to possess and use guns in public by liberalizing concealed carry laws, loosening restrictions on gun possession in bars and restaurants, and adopting of Stand Your Ground laws.[1]

But some jurisdictions — including populous states like California, New York, and New Jersey — require applicants for certain kinds of public carrying licenses to show cause (such as Maryland's "good and substantial reason"[2] or New York's "special need for self-protection"[3]) for public carrying, especially concealed public carrying. And the government interest underlying these laws is easy enough to identify, since the costs and benefits of gun use are very different in public areas than in one's home. One can support an individual right to keep and bear arms, and even support the extension of that right into public spaces, while still believing that the Second Amendment permits public carrying to constitutionally be regulated more stringently than gun possession in one's home.

Gun rights advocates have recently challenged these good cause requirements on Second Amendment grounds. If successful, their challenges could effectively compel states to issue public carrying licenses to anyone who is not a felon, mentally ill, or otherwise excluded from the scope of Second Amendment coverage. In gun law lingo, this would mean constitutionally mandating a "shall issue" regime for public carrying licenses. It is important, therefore, to understand the arguments both for and against the constitutionality of restrictions on public carrying.

The extreme position holds that any kind of good cause requirement is unconstitutional. As one district court judge put it, " citizen may not be required to offer a 'good and substantial reason' why he should be permitted to exercise his rights. The right's existence is all the reason he needs."[4] When framed this way, the point is rhetorically powerful, but substantively weak. Surely not every "cause" is "good" enough to trigger Second Amendment coverage. If a person turned in a concealed-carry application with the explanation, "I need to carry a gun in public so that I can hijack a plane with it," few would think that denying the license would violate his Second Amendment rights. It is not clear why the result would be any different if the insufficient cause were conveyed through evidence other than an outright declaration.

It follows that some good cause requirements — or at least some "not bad" cause requirements — are constitutional. Or, to put it another way, the right to keep and bear arms does not encompass a right to carry guns in public for any reason whatsoever. It is equally clear, however, that some "causes" for gun ownership are constitutionally protected, and therefore cannot be excluded by a good cause requirement. If a person (we can call him Brad) wants a gun because he is in immediate danger of being killed by violent criminals — and is not himself a felon, mentally ill, or otherwise subject to the categorical restrictions approved in District of *Columbia v. Heller*[5] — then his claim to carry a weapon in public would fall squarely within the "core" interest of self-defense.[6]

Separating these extreme cases, a host of harder questions remain. What if Brad is not actually in any danger, but simply paranoid about imagined threats? What if he wants the gun so that he can hunt squirrels, a generally lawful activity whose constitutional coverage is nevertheless unclear? What if his "bad" reason for gun ownership is not likely ever to manifest itself in illegal activity?

One partial answer to these questions is to say that self-defense is always a good cause, and that licensing regimes therefore cannot deny guns to people seeking to carry them publicly for that purpose. There is much to like in this approach. *Heller*, after all, identified self-defense as the "core" of the right to keep and bear arms.[7] And although the Court found the need for that right to be "most acute" in the home,[8] it did not explicitly limit it as such. In fact, long before *Heller*, courts recognized self-defense and necessity exceptions to gun laws,[9] even for prohibited groups like felons.[10]

But this does not necessarily mean that the Second Amendment requires that a person be able to carry a gun in public — let alone a concealed gun — any time he invokes self-defense. After all, the right of self-defense itself typically requires a person to show something like good cause — a reasonable fear of imminent harm as a result of unlawful force, for example. In other words, the core of the right to keep and bear arms is the right to keep and bear arms for self-defense; the core of the right to keep and bear arms for self-defense is self-defense. And if that core right is compatible with a good cause requirement, shouldn't the right to keep and bear arms for self-defense also be?

The difficulty of this question arises from the fact that the right to self-defense and the right to keep and bear arms for that purpose are closely related but not coextensive. When a person purchases a gun for self-defense, he generally does not know whether he will ever have to use it for that purpose — fortunately, the vast majority of gun owners never do. But in light of *Heller*, the rule cannot be that only those people who actually fire a gun in self-defense are validly exercising their Second Amendment rights.

How should the law treat the inevitable space between actions of justified self-defense and the preparations for those actions? Does the Second Amendment require the government to recognize as "good cause" a generalized claim to self-defense in the absence of a specific threat? One way to frame the issue is to ask what level of risk is necessary to "trigger" the right to carry a gun in public for purposes of self-defense. A person who is 100% certain to face a justified need for armed self-defense would surely have "good cause"; a person who is 100% certain not to have such a need would not have good cause. (The latter person could probably still have a gun at home, and might have some kind of cognizable interest in public carrying, but it is hard to see how it would be grounded in self-defense.) When does the risk become constitutionally salient? Ten percent? One percent?

Of course, people often have no way of knowing with precision the chances of their facing a "real" threat. Self-defense law and good cause requirements approach this uncertainty from two different angles. Self-defense law is about ex post risk assessment, in the sense that the event has already happened, and the law seeks to determine whether the self-defender's actions were reasonable and proportional to the threat. Good cause requirements do the same thing from an ex ante perspective, transposing the threat assessment before the action takes place.

To be sure, one might argue that reasonableness, proportionality, imminence and other "good cause" elements of self-defense should only apply to actions of self-defense, not to preparations for those actions. There is some strength to this argument as well. It is difficult to assess a risk ahead of time, which is one reason why well-tailored good cause requirements are typically more forgiving than self-defense doctrine. Thus a person seeking a license in Maryland need only show that the "permit is necessary as a reasonable precaution against apprehended danger,"[11] rather than demonstrate the "imminent or immediate danger of death or serious bodily harm"[12] necessary to justify an action of self-defense. It is also true that mere preparations for self-defense might never involve physical harm to anyone, so the state's interest in public safety is presumably lower than when it comes to actual confrontations. Nonetheless, when such preparations include the public carrying of guns, the risk of misuse is undeniable. It is that risk which good cause limitations seek to minimize.

None of this means that good cause requirements are always constitutional, only that challenges to them should focus on the details of their implementation. If a public-carry licensing regime operates like a ban, it should be evaluated as such. For the most part, though, the matter is one for legislatures to decide. These days, most of them seem to be moving in the direction of loosened restrictions. The Constitution has nothing to say about that trend. But it also has very little to say to those legislatures who have chosen to maintain a "may issue" approach to public carrying, including its attendant good cause restrictions. The Second Amendment is busy enough these days without being deployed in fights where it does not belong.

Notes

1. These and other political and legal successes make it hard to credit the analogy made by some commentators between the position of contemporary gun owners and that of black schoolchildren in the 1950s. See Alan Gura, The Second Amendment as a Normal Right, 127 HARV. L. REV. F. 223 (2014) (comparing post-Heller developments in gun rights to the struggle for racial equality after Brown v. Board of Education); David B. Kopel, Does the Second Amendment Protect Firearms Commerce?, 127 HARV. L. REV. F. 230 (2014) (same). For similar reasons, it seems inappropriate to invoke the white segregationist policy of "massive resistance" when describing lower courts' response to District of Columbia v. Heller, 554 U.S. 570 (2008). Compare Petition for Writ of Certiorari at 3, Drake v. Jerejian, No. 13-827 (U.S. Jan. 9, 2014) (describing "lower courts' massive resistance to Heller"), with WIKIPEDIA, Massive Resistance, http://en.wikipedia.org/wiki/Massive_resistance, archived at http://perma.cc/MDQ7-586A (last visited Mar. 30, 2014) (describing the "Massive Resistance" policy undertaken by white segregationists to oppose school integration).
2. MD. CODE ANN., PUB. SAFETY § 5-306(a)(6)(ii) (West 2014) (listing "necessary as a reasonable precaution against apprehended danger" among these reasons).
3. Bando v. Sullivan, 735 N.Y.S.2d 660, 662 (N.Y. App. Div. 2002) (interpreting the "proper cause" requirement of N.Y. PENAL LAW § 400.00(2)(f) (McKinney 2013)).
4. Woollard v. Sheridan, 863 F. Supp. 2d 462, 475 (D. Md. 2012), rev'd by Woollard v. Gallagher, 712 F.3d 865 (4th Cir. 2013).
5. 554 U.S. 570, 626–27 (2008) ("[[N]]othing in our opinion should be taken to cast doubt on longstanding prohibitions on the possession of firearms by felons and the mentally ill, or laws forbidding the carrying of firearms in sensitive places such as schools and government buildings, or laws imposing conditions and qualifications on the commercial sale of arms.").
6. Id. at 630.
7. Id.
8. Id. at 628.
9. State v. Hamdan, 665 N.W.2d 785, 811–12 (Wis. 2003) (creating exception in concealed carry ban for store owner whose store in a high crime neighborhood had been robbed multiple times).
10. United States v. Gomez, 81 F.3d 846, 854 (9th Cir. 1996) (finding that felon convicted for possessing a firearm should have been permitted to present a justification defense).
11. MD. CODE ANN., PUB. SAFETY § 5-306(a)(6)(ii) (West 2014).
12. State v. Faulkner, 483 A.2d 759, 761 (Md. 1984).

9

Background Checks And Mental Illness: Facts and Myths

Denise-Marie Ordway

Denise-Marie Ordway is research reporter/editor for Journalist's Resource. Ordway has been a reporter for the Orlando Sentinel and The Philadelphia Inquirer and also wrote news for two radio stations and a newspaper in Central America.

How strong is link between mental illness and violent crime? Whether individuals with a history of mental illness should be denied the right to buy a gun through stringent background checks is a frequently debated (and sometimes misunderstood) issue within the larger gun rights debate. When reporting on this sensitive and complex issue, it is essential for journalists to have the facts. Perhaps surprisingly to some, there is little data linking mental illness with violent crime. However, the high rate of suicide amongst the mentally ill suggests that background checks via the NICS system are still a good idea if applied in a manner consistent with civil liberties.

Immediately following reports that a South Florida man shot dozens of people in an Orlando nightclub in June 2016, journalists and the public began to question his mental state and mental-health history. Within days of the massacre, news agencies nationwide were reporting details about Omar Mateen's childhood, adolescence and adulthood – including behavioral problems in elementary school and his most recent online searches for information about anti-psychosis medication.

As journalists have scrutinized Mateen's life history, this latest tragedy – characterized as the worst mass shooting in U.S. history – has prompted legislators to demand stricter gun control measures and question the effectiveness of existing state and federal laws that aim to keep firearms away from individuals with mental illnesses.

Media professionals who report on these controversial issues should seek out the latest academic research in these areas and read it and understand it. Peer-reviewed research can ground journalists' coverage and allow them to differentiate facts from myths and scientific evidence from assumptions.

For many years, scholars have explored the possible ties between mental illness and violence. They have found that most people with a serious mental illness are not violent, that mental illness is not a strong risk factor for homicide. A 2014 study published by the American Psychological Association noted no predictable pattern linking criminal conduct and mental illness symptoms over time. According to the National Center for Health Statistics, fewer than 5 percent of gun-related deaths between 2001 and 2010 were caused by individuals diagnosed with a mental illness.

Below, Journalist's Resource has pulled together a sampling of research and reports that we hope will offer reporters crucial insights and also reveal new angles worth investigating:

————————————-

Gun background checks and mental illness

"Gun Violence, Mental Illness, And Laws That Prohibit Gun Possession: Evidence From Two Florida Counties"
Swanson, Jeffrey W. *Health Affairs*, June 2016, Vol. 35. doi: 10.1377/hlthaff.2016.0017.

Abstract: "Gun violence kills about 90 people every day in the United States, a toll measured in wasted and ruined lives and with an annual economic price tag exceeding $200 billion. Some policy makers suggest that reforming mental health care systems and improving point-of-purchase background checks to keep guns from mentally disturbed people will address the problem. Epidemiological research shows that serious mental illness contributes little to the risk of interpersonal violence but is a strong factor in suicide, which accounts for most firearm fatalities. Meanwhile, the effectiveness of gun restrictions focused on mental illness remains poorly understood. This article examines gun-related suicide and violent crime in people with serious mental illnesses, and whether legal restrictions on firearm sales to people with a history of mental health adjudication are effective in preventing gun violence. Among the study population in two large Florida counties, we found that 62 percent of violent gun crime arrests and 28 percent of gun suicides involved individuals not legally permitted to have a gun at the time. Suggested policy reforms include enacting risk-based gun removal laws and prohibiting guns from people involuntarily detained in short-term psychiatric hospitalizations."

"State Progress in Record Reporting for Firearm-Related Background Checks: Mental Health Submissions"

Goggins, Becki; Gallegos, Anne. Report from the U.S. Bureau of Justice Statistics, March 2016.

Abstract: "Over the past ten years, states have made vast progress in providing firearm prohibiting mental health information to the National Instant Criminal Background Check System (NICS) Index. The passage of the NICS Improvement Amendments Act (NIAA) in 2008 was a turning point in reporting; in addition to the approximately 250,000 federally-submitted mental health records, the NICS Index went from holding just over 400,000 state-submitted mental health records to over 3.8 million state-submitted records in July of 2015. This report provides an overview of legislation and reporting mechanisms for mental health information, the challenges states face in reporting, strategies that have been implemented to overcome the challenges, and finally, data that illustrate the improvements that have been accomplished over the past decade in this area."

"Preventing Persons Affected by Serious Mental Illnesses from Obtaining Firearms: The Evolution of Law, Policy, and Practice in Massachusetts"

Silver, James; Fisher, William H.; Silver, Emily. *Behavioral Sciences & the Law*, 2015, Vol. 33. doi: 10.1002/bsl.2170.

Abstract: "A history of commitment to a mental health facility disqualifies applicants for gun licenses. Identifying such a history has become increasingly complex as the locus of confinement has become more diversified and privatized. In Massachusetts, prior to 2014, the databases used to identify individuals who would be disqualified on such grounds had not contemporaneously matched the evolution of the state's mental health systems. A survey of Massachusetts police chiefs, who, as in many jurisdictions, are charged with certifying qualification, indicates that some have broadened the scope of their background checks to include the experience of their officers with respect to certain applicants. The survey identifying these patterns, conducted in 2014, preceded by one month significant legislative reforms that mandate the modification of the reporting into a centralized database commitments to all types of mental health and substance use facilities, thus allowing identification of all commitments occurring in the state. The anticipated utilization of a different database mechanism, which has parallels in several other states, potentially streamlines the background check process, but raises numerous concerns that need to be addressed in developing and using such databases."

"Mental Illness and Reduction of Gun Violence and Suicide: Bringing Epidemiologic Research to Policy"

Swanson, Jeffrey W.; McGinty, E. Elizabeth; Fazel, Seena; Mays, Vickie M. *Annals of Epidemiology*, 2015, Vol. 25. doi:10.1016/j. annepidem.2014.03.004.

Summary: This study explores the link between mental illness and violence, including suicide, as well as the effectiveness of gun-purchaser background checks in Connecticut. The Connecticut study found differences in effectiveness between two key groups: clients of the public behavioral health care system who do not have criminal records and individuals who are involved with both the criminal justice system and the behavioral health system.

"Guns, Impulsive Angry Behavior, and Mental Disorders: Results from the National Comorbidity Survey Replication (NCS-R)"

Swanson, Jeffrey W.; et al. *Behavioral Sciences & the Law*, 2015, Vol. 33. doi: 10.1002/bsl.2172.

Abstract: "Analyses from the National Comorbidity Study Replication provide the first nationally representative estimates of the co-occurrence of impulsive angry behavior and possessing or carrying a gun among adults with and without certain mental disorders and demographic characteristics. The study found that a large number of individuals in the United States self-report patterns of impulsive angry behavior and also possess firearms at home (8.9 percent) or carry guns outside the home (1.5 percent). These data document associations of numerous common mental disorders and combinations of angry behavior with gun access. Because only a small proportion of persons with this risky combination have ever been involuntarily hospitalized for a mental health problem, most will not be subject to existing mental health-related legal restrictions on firearms resulting from a history of involuntary commitment. Excluding a large proportion of the general population from gun possession is also not likely to be feasible. Behavioral risk-based approaches to firearms restriction, such as expanding the definition of gun-prohibited persons to include those with violent misdemeanor convictions and multiple DUI convictions, could be a more effective public health policy to prevent gun violence in the population."

Gun violence and mental illness

"Acts of Weapon Threat and Use Against Family Members by Persons with Psychiatric Disorders"

Labrum, Travis; Solomon, Phyllis L. *Violence and Gender*, 2016, Vol. 3. doi: 10.1089/vio.2015.0052.

Abstract: "Persons with psychiatric disorders (PD) are at a modestly increased risk of committing violence. Only a very small portion of general and gun-related violence by persons with PD is committed against strangers. Instead, family members and other well-known persons are the vast majority of such victims. The objective of the present analysis is, with the use of a U.S.-community-recruited sample, to examine rates of victimization of threats and acts of violence involving a gun or other weapon against family members committed by relatives with PD. Of the respondents, 10 percent and 4.5 percent reported that since their relative with PD was first diagnosed with a mental health condition, s/he has threatened them with a weapon and has used a weapon against them, respectively. With regard to the past 6 months, 4 percent and 2 percent of respondents reported that their relative with PD has threatened them with a weapon and used a weapon against them. It is imperative that research be conducted in this area indicating how we may best prevent acts of weapon threat and use against family members by this population. Additionally, it is important that the large part family members have in the victimization of gun and other weapon-related violence by persons with PD be acknowledged when developing social policies intended to prevent such victimization."

"Mental Illness, Mass Shootings, and the Politics of American Firearms"

Metzl, Jonathan M.; MacLeish, Kenneth T. *American Journal of Public Health*, 2015, Vol. 105. doi: 10.2105/AJPH.2014.302242.

Abstract: "Four assumptions frequently arise in the aftermath of mass shootings in the United States: (1) that mental illness causes gun violence, (2) that psychiatric diagnosis can predict gun crime, (3) that shootings represent the deranged acts of mentally ill loners, and (4) that gun control 'won't prevent' another Newtown (Connecticut school mass shooting). Each of these statements is certainly true in particular instances. Yet, as we show, notions of mental illness that emerge in relation to mass shootings frequently reflect larger cultural stereotypes and anxieties about matters such as race/ethnicity, social class, and politics. These issues become obscured when mass shootings come to stand in for all gun crime, and when 'mentally ill' ceases to be a medical designation and becomes a sign of violent threat."

"The Epidemiology of Firearm Violence in the Twenty-First Century United States"

Wintemute, Garen J. *Annual Review of Public Health*, 2015. doi: 10.1146/annurev-publhealth-031914-122535.

Abstract: "This brief review summarizes the basic epidemiology of firearm violence, a large and costly public health problem in the United States for which the mortality rate has remained unchanged for more than a decade. It presents findings for the present in light of recent trends. Risk for firearm violence varies substantially across demographic subsets of the population and between states in patterns that are quite different for suicide and homicide. Suicide is far more common than homicide and its rate is increasing; the homicide rate is decreasing. As with other important health problems, most cases of fatal firearm violence arise from large but low-risk subsets of the population; risk and burden of illness are not distributed symmetrically. Compared with other industrialized nations, the United States has uniquely high mortality rates from firearm violence."

Media coverage

"Trends in News Media Coverage Of Mental Illness In The United States: 1995–2014"

McGinty, Emma E.; Kennedy-Hendricks, Alene; Choksy, Seema; Barry, Colleen L. *Health Affairs*, June 2016, Vol. 35. doi: 10.1377/hlthaff.2016.0011.

Abstract: "The United States is engaged in ongoing dialogue around mental illness. To assess trends in this national discourse, we studied the volume and content of a random sample of 400 news stories about mental illness from the period 1995–2014. Compared to news stories in the first decade of the study period, those in the second decade were more likely to mention mass shootings by people with mental illnesses. The most frequently mentioned topic across the study period was violence (55 percent overall) divided into categories of interpersonal violence or self-directed (suicide) violence, followed by stories about any type of treatment for mental illness (47 percent). Fewer news stories, only 14 percent, described successful treatment for or recovery from mental illness. The news media's continued emphasis on interpersonal violence is highly disproportionate to actual rates of violence among those with mental illnesses. Research suggests that this focus may exacerbate social stigma and decrease support for public policies that benefit people with mental illnesses."

"Common Sense or Gun Control? Political Communication and News Media Framing of Firearm Sale Background Checks after Newtown"

McGinty, Emma E.; Wolfson, Julia A.; Sell, Tara Kirk; Webster, Daniel W. *Journal of Health Politics*, Policy and Law, 2016, Vol. 41. doi: 10.1215/03616878-3445592.

Abstract: "Gun violence is a critical public health problem in the United States, but it is rarely at the top of the public policy agenda. The 2012 mass shooting in Newtown, Connecticut, opened a rare window of opportunity to strengthen firearm policies in the United States. In this study, we examine the American public's exposure to competing arguments for and against federal- and state-level universal background check laws, which would require a background check prior to every firearm sale, in a large sample of national and regional news stories (n = 486) published in the year following the Newtown shooting. Competing messages about background check laws could influence the outcome of policy debates by shifting support and political engagement among key constituencies such as gun owners and conservatives. We found that news media messages in support of universal background checks were fact-based and used rational arguments, and opposing messages often used rights-based frames designed to activate the core values of politically engaged gun owners. Reframing supportive messages about background check policies to align with gun owners' and conservatives' core values could be a promising strategy to increase these groups' willingness to vocalize their support for expanding background checks for firearm sales."

10

Balancing Gun Rights And Public Safety On Campus

Thomas L. Harnisch

Thomas Harnisch joined AASCU in 2007 and currently serves as Director of State Relations and Policy Analysis. His research and commentary have been cited in Time Magazine, Politico, Bloomberg, *and* The Washington Post.

Advocates and critics alike tend to base their arguments about allowing concealed carry on college and university grounds on the words written in the Second Amendment. But what if this isn't an issue of the Second Amendment at all? The Second Amendment allows reasonable restrictions to guns, such as gun-free school zones. The issue of campus concealed carry is a question of public policy. Pro-gun lawmakers argue the permit holders should be allowed to carry concealed weapons for the purpose of deterring or preventing crime, but the American Association of State Colleges and Universities (AASCU) and the vast majority of students and administrators believe existing bans on weapons should remain.

I n the wake of tragic shootings on college campuses in Virginia, Illinois and elsewhere, lawmakers in 17 states have introduced measures seeking to relax concealed weapons restrictions on college and university campuses. Gun-rights advocates argue that easing

"Concealed Weapons on State College Campuses: In Pursuit of Individual Liberty and Collective Security," by Thomas L. Harnisch, American Association of State Colleges and Universities, November, 2008. Reprinted by permission.

gun restrictions could enhance both individual and collective security on campus and may deter violence. In contrast, the vast majority of college administrators, law enforcement personnel and students maintain that allowing concealed weapons on campus will pose increased risks for students and faculty, will not deter future attacks, and will lead to confusion during emergency situations. This controversial debate is expected to continue on college campuses and in statehouses throughout the nation.

Context

The tragic events at Virginia Tech and Northern Illinois University have policymakers, campus officials and citizens looking for solutions to prevent future attacks. Violent shootings that have occurred on a few college campuses in recent years have provoked a debate over the best ways to ensure the safety of students, faculty and staff. Lawmakers in several states have advanced the idea allowing citizens with concealed weapons permits to carry their weapons on campus. The term "weapons" usually refer to handguns, but in some instances may refer to other self-defense tools such as knives, stun guns and billy clubs. These legislative proposals have been met with considerable controversy, evoking strong emotion on both sides. Thus far, Utah is the only state to have adopted this policy. All other state legislatures where similar bills have been introduced have rejected the idea.

The Second Amendment—the right to keep and bear arms as established by the U.S. Constitution and many state constitutions—is not at issue in this controversy. Rather, this is a policy debate over how best to ensure public safety, as the Second Amendment is subject to reasonable restrictions, such as bans on guns in schools. The majority opinion of the U.S. Supreme Court recently concluded in *District of Columbia vs. Heller*:

> Although we do not undertake an exhaustive historical analysis today of the full scope of the Second Amendment, nothing in our opinion should be taken to cast doubt on longstanding prohibitions on the possession of firearms by felons and the

mentally ill, or laws forbidding the carrying of firearms in sensitive places such as schools and government buildings, or laws imposing conditions and qualifications on the commercial sale of arms.

The majority also noted: "We identify these presumptively lawful regulatory measures only as examples; our list does not purport to be exhaustive." While striking down the District of Columbia's strict ban on handguns, the justices did not call into question any of the existing gun bans on college campuses.

Likewise, state constitutions affirming the right to keep and bear arms have not cast campus gun bans in doubt. Concealed weapons bans on college campuses have not been challenged under these longstanding provisions and no court has ever struck down a campus firearms restriction, whether imposed under state law or administrative policy.

Observations

Currently, nearly all public colleges and universities ban student possession of concealed weapons on campus through state laws, university regulations or both. In approximately 26 states, state law prohibits guns on public college campuses, even for people that have obtained concealed weapons licenses, with the exception of university public safety officers. Only one state, Utah, prohibits its state institutions from barring guns on campus.

Twenty-three states allow public campuses or state systems to determine their own weapons policies, with nearly all choosing to be "gun-free." Colorado State University (CSU) is an exception, but the campus still retains some restrictions. Some colleges and universities allow guns within campus boundaries for off-campus hunting activities, but campus officials usually require hunters to secure firearms in locked campus facilities.

Private colleges are usually allowed to create their own regulations in conformity with state concealed weapons laws. Utah, while prohibiting public colleges from barring guns, allows private colleges the autonomy to devise their own policies. However, in

2009 some state legislatures are likely to introduce legislation aimed at stripping both public and private colleges of the right to regulate weapons on campus.

State laws vary considerably with respect to allowing weapons on campus. Wyoming, for example, prohibits guns unless the person has the permission of campus security officials. Other states specifically disallow guns in classrooms and dormitories, while others provide exceptions for guns in automobiles. Two states, Wisconsin and Illinois, have outright bans on concealed weapons statewide, thus including colleges and universities. Finally, some states do not address guns on campus in state law, but because they seldom issue concealed-weapons permits, university-imposed regulations are a non-issue.

Current state concealed weapons laws and campus regulations are being challenged in state legislatures. In some states, legislation will be introduced in 2009 that would permit all colleges and universities, both public and private, to allow concealed weapons on campus. However, in most states, it is anticipated that the proposed legislation would limit the possession of handguns on public college and university campuses to faculty, staff or students enrolled in the Reserve Officer Training Corps (R.O.T.C.) program.

In all, 17 states attempted major reforms to campus weapon laws in 2008: Alabama, Arizona, Georgia, Idaho, Indiana, Kentucky, Louisiana, Michigan, Minnesota, Mississippi, Ohio, Oklahoma, South Dakota, South Carolina, Tennessee, Virginia and Washington. In addition, Texas lawmakers, with the backing of Gov. Rick Perry (R), are considering introducing similar weapon reform legislation. When state legislatures reconvene in 2009, campus weapon regulations promise to be a controversial topic for political leaders, students and university personnel.

Recent efforts have not yielded any victories for gun-rights advocates, in part because college administrators, law enforcement personnel and students have vehemently spoken out against the proposals. Polling also suggests, among students and non-students alike, that allowing guns on campus is unpopular. In

2001, a Harvard School of Public Health survey indicated that the vast majority (94 percent) of people believe citizens should not be allowed to carry guns onto college campuses. A survey of Missouri State University students, conducted in April 2008, found that only 24 percent of respondents believed students should be allowed to carry guns on the Missouri State campus. Mike Robinson, Oklahoma State University director of public safety, echoed this sentiment in comments he made regarding a state measure to ease campus gun laws: "Students don't want it. Faculty doesn't want it. Administration doesn't want it. Campuses are one of the safest places you can be. I am certain that campuses will be less safe if we allow guns."

On one side of the controversy, gun-rights advocates argue that existing campus weapon restrictions do not allow for individual self- protection and may contribute to loss of life. Students for Concealed Carry on Campus (SCCC), a gun-rights advocacy group, contend that students with gun permits should be "afforded the same right to carry on college campuses that they are currently afforded virtually everywhere else." For example, employees and students at colleges and universities often have to work late and then walk to their homes, automobiles or bus stops off campus in unsafe areas. The group contends that preventing these individuals from carrying a concealed weapon reduces their ability to protect themselves from would-be attackers once off campus.

Second, advocates for allowing concealed weapons on campus maintain that students, staff and faculty should have the right to self-protection in the event of a violent campus attack such as the one that occurred in April 2007 at Virginia Tech. Proponents of easing gun laws on campus argue that the victims at Virginia Tech were left with little recourse, as they did not have the right to possess weapons to defend themselves. They contend that current gun regulations limit bystanders' options to protect themselves in the event of a future attack.

Similarly, advocates maintain that armed and trained individuals could potentially save lives in a situation similar to

Virginia Tech. The SCCC group argues that it is "now abundantly clear that 'gun free zones' serve to disarm only those law-abiding citizens who might be able to mitigate such tragedies." In recent instances of gun violence, police charged with protecting the campus could not arrive soon enough to stop the massacres.

Third, gun-rights advocates contend that carrying concealed weapons could potentially deter campus attacks and lessen campus crime. Current regulations restricting firearms on campus have not deterred recent attacks, and some gun-rights advocates believe that would-be attackers might reconsider their actions if they knew students or faculty were allowed to possess weapons. Louisiana State Rep. Earnest Wooten pointed out, "We've got a problem and maybe it'll be a deterrent if one of those disturbed persons or whackos thinks, 'If I go in shooting, they may shoot back.'"

In a broader sense, some researchers reason that greater possession of concealed weapons will translate into less crime. Drs. John Lott and David B. Mustard, two leading researchers on gun and crime issues, conclude: "Allowing citizens without criminal records or histories of significant mental illness to carry concealed handguns deters violent crimes and appears to produce an extremely small and statistically insignificant change in accidental deaths." Their studies, praised by gun right advocates, have been used to justify liberalizing state gun laws restrictions, including the effort to allow concealed weapons on campus.

Conversely, most college administrators, law enforcement personnel, students, gun-control advocates and editorial boards have expressed serious reservations about allowing concealed weapons on campus. Foremost in their reasoning is that the challenges that are often inherent in college life (including drug use, alcohol abuse, stress and social obstacles), when overlapped with weapons, could have potentially lethal consequences for all people in the campus community. Given these stresses, opponents argue that introducing guns onto college campuses may increase the safety risks to students, faculty and staff. The presence of firearms could lead to conflicts between roommates, classmates and others on campus, escalating to the point where one or more individuals could be injured or killed as a result of gun violence. As Bill King, chief of public safety at Florida International University suggests, "Students having weapons on campus could make a volatile situation worse." The presence of these weapons may also invite gun theft; resulting in potential misuse and exacerbating the likelihood that physical harm would ensue.

The availability of weapons on campus could also have an adverse impact on the student suicide rate. According to the Suicide Prevention Network, suicide is the second leading cause of death for American college students, and thousands more attempt suicide and do not succeed. Easy access to firearms on campus would likely worsen this serious problem, as suicide attempts involving

firearms are almost always successful. Studies show that having firearms in the household correlates with a greater risk of successful suicide. Opponents of easing campus gun laws contend that allowing access to firearms in student residence halls and on-campus apartments would provide an efficient and convenient method of suicide during a momentary mental health crisis, and thus increase the likelihood of additional human tragedy.

Second, campus police and security personnel are concerned about inappropriate responses during emergency situations. While police are extensively trained to deal with crises, students or university staff with concealed weapons permits are not trained or integrated into campus security plans. Even with the best of intentions, armed students or employees could escalate an already explosive situation further, accidentally cause harm or use a gun in a situation that is not warranted.

Likewise, police could mistake the attacker for an armed student or employee (or vice versa) during a situation in which failure to make quick, discernible judgments can be extraordinarily costly for all parties involved. In a *Christian Science Monitor* article (05/18/07) on the guns on campus debate, Dana Schrad, the executive director of the Virginia Association of Chiefs of Police, said, "I have my own concerns that, had there been a number of people who had been in that classroom with guns, [there could have been] additional persons killed just as a result of poor judgment calls."

Third, the hypothetical correlation between the presence of guns and crime deterrence as a justification for expanding areas where guns can be carried has been called into question by leading scholars. Ian Ayres of Yale Law School and John J. Donohue III of Stanford Law School refute data and contentions made by Drs. Lott and Mustard, arguing, "Statistical evidence that these laws have reduced crime is limited, sporadic and extraordinarily fragile." They continue, "If anything, there is stronger evidence for the conclusion that these laws increase crime than there is for the conclusion that they decrease it."

Others argue that "deterrence" of mentally disturbed individuals is simply unrealistic. Opponents of the argument believe changes in weapons laws will not prevent people with mental disorders from proceeding with violent plans. Josh Horwitz of the Coalition to Stop Gun Violence wrote for *The New York Times* (05/16/08), "Most mass shooters are suicidal; they intended to die. Armed confrontation is not a deterrent, it is the point."

Fourth, potential liability and administrative costs need to be considered by policymakers. Colleges are expected to provide a reasonable level of safety to students, faculty and staff. Liberalizing gun laws would deprive colleges of the discretion to set restrictions concerning firearms, thus exposing them to potential liability without the means to establish sensible policies to reduce risks. The Brady Center to Prevent Gun Violence cites a number of cases in which colleges and universities have been held liable for shootings, suicides and other violent acts.

Administrative costs may bring an additional financial burden to campus police. According to the International Association of Campus Law Enforcement Administrators, if firearms are allowed on campus, police may need to investigate firearm incidents and firearm theft, as well as regulate age requirements. This could be a sizable and unnecessary distraction for campus law enforcement personnel, with the associated costs adding to already mounting fiscal pressures faced by departments and universities.

Fifth, institutional autonomy is a key issue in the debate over control of weapons policies at schools. State constitutions grant administrative autonomy to either system or institutional governing boards that oversee public colleges and universities.

Stripping them of the ability to regulate guns on campus could be construed as an unconstitutional infringement on this autonomy.

Finally, private colleges also have private property rights. Legislation introduced in some states would strip these colleges of their rights to regulate guns on their campuses. State legislation either barring or mandating an allowance for concealed weapons on private college campuses could be construed as an intrusion on private property rights.

Conclusion

American public college and university campuses have long served as venues in which individual rights are championed. At the same time, however, the safety and security of all members of the campus community must remain paramount. As state lawmakers deliberate over allowing concealed weapons on campus, they should consider the following:

- The potential impact of guns given the dynamics of the college campus environment
- Responses during campus emergencies
- The actual likelihood of criminal deterrence
- The associated potential liability and administrative costs
- Federal and state constitutional issues, including individual rights and institutional autonomy

Recent tragedies demonstrate that campuses must be vigilant in identifying potential threats and develop coherent security strategies to effectively prepare for campus crises. Lawmakers must consider all consequences, both intended and unintended, of allowing concealed weapons on state college campuses.

Given the overriding goal to ensure that campuses are safe environments, the American Association of State Colleges and Universities (AASCU) maintains support for existing state laws that ban concealed weapons from public college campuses, or that provide for institutional and system autonomy with regard to concealed weapons policy. Further, the association discourages the passage of new state legislation that would overturn or weaken concealed weapons bans on campus.

The issue of how best to uphold the individual right to self-protection while ensuring collective security on campus will continue to generate considerable public discussion. It is a debate that is certain to remain vigorous and one that will challenge public safety officials, campus leaders and lawmakers alike.

Resources

Brady Center to Prevent Gun Violence. *No Gun Left Behind: The Gun Lobby's Campaign to Push Guns Into Colleges and Schools* (2007) and *The Case Against Guns on Campus* (2007) outline the rationale behind keeping guns off college and university campuses. The sister organization, Brady Campaign to Prevent Gun Violence, maintains a website with up-to-date facts, links to recent news articles, and a map of states where legislation has been introduced.
http://www.bradycampaign.org/xshare/pdf/reports/
no-gun-left-behind.pdf
http://www.law.gmu.edu/gmucrlj/docs/seibel.doc http://www.bradycampaign.org/
gunsoncampus

Colorado State University. *Handguns on Campus: Do you have the facts?* A brochure describing CSU's regulations regarding guns on campus.
http://publicsafety.colostate.edu/WeaponsBrochure.pdf

Gary Brinker-Missouri State University. *Survey of Missouri State University Students' Opinions on Carrying Guns on Campus* (2008). Offers polling results of the views of carrying guns on the Missouri State campus.
http://www.news-leader.com/assets/pdf/DO109012522.PDF

John Lott and David Mustard. *Crime, Deterrence, and the Right-to-Carry Handguns* utilizes empirical data to correlate deterrence in crime associated with increased gun ownership.
http://homepage.usask.ca/~sta575/cdn-firearms/Lott/lott.pdf

Ian Ayres and John J. Donohue III. *Shooting down the "More Guns, Less Crime Hypothesis* challenges the conclusions of John Lott and David Mustard.
http://islandia.law.yale.edu/ayers/Ayres_Donohue_article.pdf

International Association of Campus Law Enforcement Officers (IACLEA). The IACLEA provides resources on campus safety and has adopted a position on concealed carry on campus.
http://www.iaclea.org/visitors/PDFs/ ConcealedWeaponsStatement_Aug2008.pdf

Guns: Conceal and Carry

Harvard School of Public Health. *Guns and Gun Threats at College* (2001). Describes attitudes towards guns on campuses.
http://www.hsph.harvard.edu/cas/Documents/Gunthreats2/ gunspdf.pdf

Legal Community Against Violence offers legal assistance in support of gun violence prevention.
http://www.lcav.org/

National Rifle Association (NRA). The NRA promotes gun ownership rights.
http://www.nra.org/

Students for Concealed Carry on Campus (SCCC). The SCCC believes students should have the right to carry concealed weapons on public college campuses.
www.concealedcampus.org

Supreme Court of the United States. *District of Columbia vs. Heller* (2008) states the Court's ruling on a key Second Amendment case.
http://www.supremecourtus.gov/opinions/07pdf/07-290.pdf

11

Students May Threaten Professors for Better Grades

Jessica Smartt Gullion

Jessica Smartt Gullion, PhD, is Assistant Professor of Sociology at Texas Woman's University. She is the author of more than 20 peer-reviewed articles, in journals such as Qualitative Inquiry, the International Review of Qualitative Research, and the Journal of Applied Social Science.

As previously mentioned, the state of Texas has passed legislation permitting the presence of firearms in previously-restricted areas of college campuses, including inside classrooms. The following viewpoint, written before the law went into effect, imagines the physical dangers to students and professors inherent in this decision. Another, perhaps secondary, concern is that university instructors will be coerced into assigning better, unearned grades against the threat of physical harm of a student who has a gun. Rates if mental illness, depression, and high-stakes pressure are very high on college campuses. Is it responsible to put at risk those people whose responsibility is to educate the next generation?

Texas college professors may soon face a dilemma between upholding professional ethics and protecting their lives.

On Thursday, December 10, a task force at the University of Texas at Austin recommended restricting guns in residence halls, at sporting events and in certain laboratories, but allowed them in classrooms.

The 19-member task force was set up following a "Campus Carry" law passed by the state in Spring 2015. The law, which will come into effect on August 1, 2016, will allow people with handgun licenses to carry concealed firearms on college campuses.

With the recommendation to allow firearms in classrooms, a question coming up for many academics is whether they would be forced to give As to undeserving students, just so they can avoid being shot.

This is not as far fetched as it sounds. In my five years as a college professor, I have had experience with a number of emotionally distressed students who resort to intimidation when they receive a lesser grade than what they feel they deserve.

Threats on campus

Here is an example of one such threatening experience: one evening in a graduate course, after I handed back students' papers, a young woman stood up and pointed at me. "This is unacceptable!" she screamed as her body shook in rage.

She moved toward the front of the class waving her paper in my face and screamed again, "unacceptable!" After a heated exchange, she left the room, and stood outside the door sobbing.

All this was over receiving a B on a completely low-stakes assignment.

What followed was even more startling. The following week, the student brought along a muscle-bound man to class. He watched me through the doorway window for the entire three hours of the class, with his arms folded across his chest.

And if this wasn't enough, the young woman's classmates avoided me on campus because, they said, they were afraid of getting caught in the crossfire should she decide to shoot me.

After that, every time she turned in a paper I cringed and prayed that it was good so that I wouldn't have to give her anything less than an A.

Learning from this experience, now I give papers back only at the end of the class or just "forget" to bring them with me.

I was lucky that the student didn't have a gun in my classroom. Other professors have not been so lucky.

In 2014 a student at Purdue shot his instructor in front of a classroom of students. In another incident in 2009, a student at Northern Virginia Community College tried to shoot his math professor on campus. And, in 2000, a graduate student at the University of Arkansas shot his English professor.

In each of these states, carrying handguns on campus was illegal at the time of the shooting, although a bill was introduced in Arkansas earlier this year to allow students to carry guns.

Grade inflation

Despite these and other shootings, a new trend has emerged across the US that supports guns on college campuses.

Nine states allow firearms onto college campuses and 11 states are now considering similar legislation.

We know that some students will carry guns whether it is legal or not. One study found that close to five percent of undergraduates had a gun on campus and that almost two percent had been threatened with a firearm while at school.

Allowing students to carry weapons to class strips off a layer of safety. Students are often emotional and can be volatile when it comes to their GPAs.

Who would want to give a student a low grade and then get shot for it?

Many majors are highly competitive and require certain GPAs for admission. Students on scholarships and other forms of financial aid must maintain high grades to keep their funding. It's no surprise that some might students resort to any means necessary to keep up their GPAs.

An international student once cried in my office and begged me to change his F to an A, as without it, his country would no longer pay for him to be in the US. I didn't. He harassed me by posting threatening messages on Facebook.

So, the question is, will we soon see a new sort of grade inflation, with students earning a 4.0 GPA with their firepower rather than brain power? And if so, what sort of future citizenry will we be building on our campuses?

12

More Gun Availability Means More Crime

Irshad Altheimer

Irshad Altheimer is Associate Professor of Criminal Justice at Rochester Institute of Technology, and the Deputy Director of the Center for Public Safety Initiatives (CPSI).

The relationship between guns on the streets and crime rates is a complex and tangled one. Do more guns increase or deter crime? Or are these relationships independent, relying on more complex sociological factors? It can be argued that most of the evidence supports an association between more guns and more violence. This conclusion refutes the previous viewpoint. Indeed, the article cites Lott's study, but also notes that that study has seen much critical scrutiny. Although these studies increase our understanding, our knowledge of this relationship is incomplete, since national data is difficult to accurately obtain.

Abstract

This study examines the relationship between gun availability and crime in a cross-national sample of cities. Data from the International Crime Victimization Survey are used to examine three competing hypotheses. The results of the limited information maximum least squares regression analyses suggest that gun availability influences rates of assault, gun assault, robbery, and gun robbery. These findings suggest that increasing city levels of gun availability in this cross-national sample of cities increases

"An Exploratory Analysis of Guns and Violent Crime in a Cross-National Sample of Cities", by Irshad Altheimer, Southwestern Association of Criminal Justice, Vol. 6 (3), 2010, pp. 204-227. Reprinted by permission.

the likelihood that violent crimes are committed and that guns are involved in these crimes. Importantly, these findings do not suggest that increasing gun availability reduces crime.

Introduction

The relationship between guns and violent crime is an intensely debated topic. Competing theoretical claims have emerged that view guns as a cause of violent crime, a mechanism to reduce violent crime, or totally unrelated to violent crime. Myriad criminological studies have been published over the years concerning this relationship, but no clear consensus has emerged. For example, some studies have found a significant relationship between gun availability and homicide (Cook & Ludwig, 2006; Hoskin, 2001; Kleck, 1979; McDowall, 1991) while others have not (Kleck, 1984; Kleck & Patterson, 1993; Magaddino & Medoff, 1984). Additionally, at least one controversial study has found that increasing gun availability will reduce crime (Lott, 2000), but this study has come under considerable scrutiny, and its results have been challenged (Ludwig, 1998; Maltz & Targoniski, 2002; Martin & Legault, 2005; Rubin & Dezhbakhsh, 2003; Zimring & Hawkins, 1997). As such, the debate about the relationship between guns and crime at the macro level rages on.

A body of cross-national research has emerged that attempts to inform the debate about the relationship between gun availability and violent crime. Most of this research has found a significant association between gun availability and violence (Hemenway & Miller, 2000; Hoskin, 2001; Killias, 1993; Killias, van Kesteren, & Rindlisbacher, 2001; Krug, Powell, & Dahlberg, 1998; Lester, 1991). Although findings from these studies have increased knowledge on this topic, our understanding of it is incomplete because many questions about the relationship between guns and violent crime at the cross-national level have gone unanswered. For instance, virtually all of the existing cross-national studies on this topic have examined homicide as the dependent variable. As such, little is known about how gun availability and violent crime operate in a cross-national context when crimes besides homicide are considered. Additionally, most studies have examined data from Western Developed nations and examined the nation state as the unit of analysis. This has limited what is known about the nature of the gun/crime relationship when levels of analysis besides the nation are explored and when data from nations besides Western Developed nations are examined. Further, only one existing cross-national study has accounted for potential simultaneity between gun availability and crime (Hoskin, 2001), thereby begging the question of whether significant associations between gun availability and crime indicate that gun availability affects crime or vice versa?

There are both theoretical and empirical justifications for addressing the questions raised above. First, theorists on both sides of the gun/crime debate have argued that gun availability can influence crimes other than homicide. For example, Lott (2000) has suggested that increasing gun availability can reduce overall levels of crime by enabling potential victims to deter or disrupt the actions of potential aggressors. Second, there is a small body of empirical research that has shown that gun availability is associated with crimes other than homicide. For instance, Cook (1979) found that gun availability was highly correlated with gun robbery in a sample of American cities. Third, there is evidence that some predictors of crime operate differently to influence crime at different levels of analysis (Land, McCall, & Cohen, 1990). All of the previous cross-national research on gun availability and violent crime has examined nation-level data. Thus, it is plausible that the significant association between gun availability and violent crime that has been found at the nation level does not hold at the city level. Finally, there is some evidence that the effects of some macro-predictors on crime vary across different types of societies. For example, Rosenfeld and Messner (1991) found that the effect of economic inequality on homicide is not generalizable across different types of societies. Economic inequality, one of the most powerful predictors of homicide in Western Developed nations, was not found to influence homicide in a sample of small, non-industrial societies. Existing research that has examined the relationship between gun availability and crime using cities as the level of analysis primarily has focused on the United States (Fischer, 1969; Kleck & Patterson, 1993; McDowall, 1991). It is plausible that the findings from these studies are not generalizable to different social settings.

Taken together, these points suggest that research that explores the association between guns and crime at a level of analysis that has not previously been explored, for types of crime that have not yet been examined, and using data that have not previously been considered is warranted. Towards that end, the objective of this paper is to explore the association between gun availability—as measured by household gun ownership levels—and assault, gun assault, robbery, and gun robbery in a cross-national sample of thirty-nine cities primarily located in nations in transition and developing nations. Using data from the International Crime Victimization Survey (ICVS), this study employs limited information maximum least squares regression analysis to test three competing hypotheses that account for the relationship between gun availability and rates of crime.

Theory

No dominant theoretical perspective exists that explains the relationship between gun ownership and crime. The basis for such a perspective, however, has been proposed by Kleck and McElrath (1991) who suggest that weapons are a source of power used instrumentally to achieve goals by inducing compliance with the user's demands. The goals of a potential gun user are numerous and could include money, sexual gratification, respect, attention, or domination. Notably, most of these goals can be achieved by brandishing a gun but not necessarily discharging one. Unlike most criminological research, which assumes that the possession of weapons is inherently violence enhancing (i.e., Zimring, 1968; 1972), Kleck (1997) suggests that guns can confer power to both a potential aggressor and a potential victim seeking to resist aggression. When viewed in this manner, several hypotheses can be derived concerning the relationship between gun availability and crime. This first is that increasing gun availability increases total rates of crime and rates of gun crime. The second is that increasing gun avail- ability reduces crime rates. A third hypothesis is that gun availability and crime are unrelated.

Hypothesis 1: Increasing Gun Availability Increases Crime

Theoretical perspectives have emerged that suggest that gun availability increases both total crime rates and gun crime rates. The facilitation and triggering hypotheses focus primarily on the effects of gun availability on total crime rates, while the instrumentality hypothesis focuses primarily on the substitution of guns for other weapons during the commission of a crime and the implications that this has for gun crime rates.

The facilitation hypothesis suggests that increasing gun availability can increase total rates of assault and robbery when the availability of a gun provides encouragement to someone considering an attack or to someone who normally would not commit an attack. This encouragement is derived from the fact that the possession of a gun can enhance the power of a potential aggressor, thereby ensuring compliance from a victim, increasing the chances that the crime will be successfully completed, and reducing the likelihood that an actual physical attack (as opposed to a threat) will be necessary. This is particularly important in situations when the aggressor is smaller or weaker than the victim. In such cases, the aggressor's possession of a gun can neutralize the size and strength advantage of an opponent (Cook, 1982; Felson, 1996; Kleck, 1997). Guns can also facilitate crime by emboldening an aggressor who would normally avoid coming into close contact with a victim or using a knife or blunt object to stab or bludgeon someone to death. An additional way that guns can increase crime is by triggering aggression of a potential offender. This "weapons effect" is said to occur because angry people are likely to associate guns with aggressive behavior (Berkowitz & Lepage, 1967). Similarly, it has been suggested that the presence of a gun is likely to intensify negative emotions such as anger (Berkowitz, 1983).

When applied to the macro-level, the facilitation and triggering hypotheses suggest a positive association between gun availability and both the gun violence rates and total violence rates. Gun availability would be expected to have a positive association with gun assault and gun robbery because greater access to guns would lead more citizens of a respective city to believe that a crime can be successfully facilitated if a gun is used. Additionally, gun availability is expected to be positively associated with overall levels of assault and robbery because the availability of guns will trigger aggression among citizens of a respective city and encourage individuals who normally would not commit a crime to do so.

The weapon instrumentality hypothesis suggests that gun availability can increase the likelihood that gun crimes are committed. This occurs when increasing gun availability increases the likelihood that an aggressor substitutes a gun for another weapon or no weapon at all during the commission of a crime. The end result is the intensification of violence (Cook, 1991; Zimring & Hawkins, 1997). The basic premise of the weapon instrumentality perspective is that the use of a gun during the commission of an assault or robbery (1) increases the likelihood of death or serious injury; (2) provides aggressors with the opportunity to inflict injury at long distances; and (3) makes it easier to assault multiple victims than the use of other weapons that are commonly used to commit violent crime (i.e., knife or bat).

When applied to the macro-level, the weapon instrumentality hypothesis suggests that gun availability will be positively associated with gun violence. Increasing gun availability levels in a city will lead more city residents to substitute guns for other weapons during the commission of aggressive acts. In such situations, these crimes may be more likely to lead to death or violent injury. Notably, the weapon instrumentality hypothesis does not suggest that increasing gun availability increases total rates of assault and robbery. From this perspective, the substitution of a gun for another weapon does not necessarily increase the likelihood that an assault or robbery will be committed (although it may increase the likelihood that a homicide is committed), but it does increase the chances that the crimes that are committed involve guns.

Hypothesis 2: Increasing Gun Availability Reduces Crime

Another perspective on this issue suggests that the availability of guns actually can reduce levels of crime (Cook, 1991; Kleck, 1997; Lott, 2000; Lott & Mustard, 1997). From this perspective, increased levels of gun availability empower the general public to disrupt or deter criminal aggression (Cook, 1991; Kleck, 1997). Kleck (1997) suggests that gun availability can disrupt criminal aggression in two ways. First, an armed victim can prevent the completion of a crime by neutralizing the power of an armed aggressor or by shifting the balance of power in favor of the victim when confronted by an unarmed aggressor (Kleck, 1997; Kleck & Delone, 1993; Tark & Kleck, 2004). Second, an armed victim can use a weapon to resist offender aggression and avoid injury (Kleck, 1997).

Increased levels of gun availability may also reduce crime by deterring potential aggressors (Kleck, 1997; Wright & Rossi, 1986). Aggressors may refrain from committing crime due to fear of violent retaliation from victims. This deterrence can be both specific and general. For instance, a criminal may refrain from committing future attacks because they were confronted with an armed victim during a previous experience. Alternatively, an aggressor may refrain from committing a criminal act if they believe that a large proportion of the pool of potential victims is armed (Rengert & Wasilchick, 1985). When applied to the macro-level, this perspective suggests that gun availability should be negatively associated with both gun crime and crime. This is because in cities where residents have greater access to guns, potential victims will be better able to deter or disrupt the acts of criminal aggressors.

Hypothesis 3: Increasing Gun Availability
Does Not Influence Crime

The third perspective discussed here suggests that gun availability has no overall effect on levels of crime (Kleck, 1997). The absence of an effect can be the result of two things. First, gun availability simply may not influence crime. From this perspective, the use of a gun simply may reflect an aggressor's greater motivation to seriously harm a victim (Wolfgang, 1958). If true, lack of access to a gun will simply cause an aggressor to substitute another weapon to achieve a desired outcome. Second, an effect between gun availability and crime may not be detected because defensive gun use may offset the effects of guns being used for criminal aggression (Kleck, 1997). That is, any relationship might be canceled out by offsetting or opposite effects. When applied to the macro-level, this perspective suggests that changes in the gun availability of a respective city will not influence or be associated with crime in that city.

[...]

Results

Results for the analyses performed in this study are reported in Tables 1 and 2 [not reproduced]. Table 1 reports descriptive statistics and bivariate correlations for the variables used in the analysis. These correlations suggest that gun availability is positively associated with all of the crime indicators, thereby lending support to the weapon facilitation and instrumentality hypotheses. In addition, the results from Table 1 indicate that the gun availability indicator has a significant positive association with residents' concern about crime. This suggests that residents of these cities may purchase guns when they believe that their homes are at-risk of being burglarized.

The bivariate correlations reported in Table 1 also find some notable relationships between crime and many of the exogenous variables. The age structure variable is significantly associated with three of the four crime variables. In addition, unemployment is associated with gun robbery. None of the other control variables are significantly associated with crime. Taken together, these correlation coefficients suggest that gun availability and crime are associated, but a more sophisticated analysis is needed to address issues of causality and model simultaneity.

Table 2 reports stages one and two of the LIML regression analysis examining the relation- ship between gun availability and assault, gun assault, robbery, and gun robbery. As mentioned above, stage one of the analysis involves regressing gun availability on the exogenous predictors of crime. This is done to create an instrumental variable that is highly correlated with actual levels of gun availability but not correlated with the error terms of any of the crime indicators. Stage two of the analysis involves substituting the instrumental variable for the actual gun availability measure in an analysis of the effects of gun availability on crime. Because this study is interested in four separate crime variables, the results reported in stage two of Table 2 include models that examine the effects of the predicted gun availability variable on assault, gun assault, robbery, and gun robbery, respectively.

I begin the discussion with the effects of gun availability on assault. The results reveal that gun availability positively influences rates of assault in this sample of cities. This finding lends support to the facilitation hypothesis. In addition, sex ratio, age structure, and family disruption were found to positively affect levels of assault. One surprising finding is that individuals who report going out on a nightly basis are less likely to be victims of assault. This finding is opposite of what might be expected. One potential explanation is that the violence indicator used here taps into rates of domestic assault. If this is the case, it is plausible that some residents are safer outside of the home because leaving the home provides refuge from violent domestic disputes. Overall the model is robust, with 55% of the variation in assault being explained.

The results reported in Table 2 also reveal that gun availability influences gun assault. This finding lends support to the weapon instrumentality hypothesis. As levels of gun availability increase in this sample of cities, the rate of assaults involving guns also increases. This finding suggests that increasing the availability of guns increases the likelihood that a gun, as opposed to another weapon or no weapon at all, will be used in an assault. In all, 14% of the variation in gun assault is explained in this model.

I now turn to the effects of gun availability on robbery and gun robbery. The models examined are also reported in Table 2. The results reveal that gun availability influences both robbery and gun robbery. These findings also lend support to both the weapon instrumentality and facilitation hypotheses. Age structure and family disruption influenced robbery victimization while sex ratio was found to influence gun robbery. Both the robbery and gun robbery models are relatively robust. Thirty-seven percent of the variation in robbery, and 35% of the variation in gun robbery was explained by the models examined here.

[...]

13

Explaining Mass Shootings

John Wihbey

John Wihbey is an assistant professor of journalism and new media at Northeastern University, where he teaches in the Media Innovation program and is a faculty member with the NULab for Texts, Maps, and Networks.

While the murder rate has decreased overall since 1991, the United States still has a higher rate of murder than other countries of a comparable socio-economic status. More troublesome still, the number of mass shootings, sometimes referred to as "rampages," has doubled in the past decade. Some the recent literature can shed light on this disturbing phenomenon. Some texts such as James L. Knoll's The 'Pseudocommando' Mass Murderer: Part I, The Psychology of Revenge and Obliteration *provide a psychological profile of these perpetrators. Other books such as* Murder by Numbers: Monetary Costs Imposed by a Sample of Homicide Offenders *examine the issue from a broader societal perspective.*

Sandy Hook, Aurora, the Washington Navy Yard, Fort Hood, and Emanuel African Methodist Episcopal Church in Charleston, S.C. These place names signify terrible tragedies that continue to prompt deep reflection from policymakers and the public about how to stop acts of mass violence in the United States.

While FBI statistics show that levels of violent crime in the United States, including murder, have steadily declined since 1991, acts of murder and non-negligent manslaughter still claim about 15,000 lives a year. More than half of all such violent crimes in a given year are typically committed with guns. Over the past 30 years, public mass shootings have resulted in the murder of 547 people, with 476 other persons injured, according to a March 2013 Congressional Research Service report. "[W]hile tragic and shocking," the report notes, "public mass shootings account for few of the murders or non-negligent homicides related to firearms that occur annually in the United States." For more on these dynamics, see the May 2013 Pew Research Center report titled "Gun Homicide Rate Down 49% Since 1993 Peak; Public Unaware."

Even as the total gun homicide rate has fallen, however, some of the worst acts of violence in U.S. history have taken place within the past decade. Half of the deadliest shootings — incidents at Virginia Tech, Aurora, Sandy Hook, Binghamton, Fort Hood (2009), the Washington Navy Yard and a church in Charleston — have taken place since 2007. In September 2014 the FBI released a report confirming that U.S. mass shootings had risen sharply since 2007: From 2000 to 2006, there were an average of 6.4 annually; from 2007 to 2013, the average more than doubled, rising to 16.4 such shootings per year.

As a 2011 United Nations report notes, America has a "relatively high homicide rate compared to other countries with a similar socio-economic level," but per-capita homicide rates in the Caribbean, Central America and Africa are often much higher and approach "crisis" levels there. The relationship between gun availability and homicide rates is, according to an *American Journal of Criminal Justice* paper, "not stable across nations." Even so, a 2011 study in the *Journal of Trauma*compared the United States with similar nations and found that U.S. homicide rates were "6.9 times higher than rates in the other high-income countries, driven by firearm homicide rates that were 19.5 times higher. For

15-year olds to 24-year olds, firearm homicide rates in the United States were 42.7 times higher than in the other countries."

For more on the relationship between firearm ownership and homicide rates, see this review for the National Academy of Sciences (more below), as well as this study in the *American Journal of Public Health*. There are multiple important questions about deterrence, restrictions, access to guns and criminal justice interventions that have yet to be resolved, as a group of the country's leading researchers in the field concluded in 2007. Still, Australia's experience with increased gun regulation, as detailed in a study in *Injury Prevention*, suggests that some laws in certain contexts can reduce firearm violence. The findings of research on the 1994 assault weapons ban and its effects are reviewed here.

For an overview of the technical and legal aspects of firearms and ammunition in the United States — and a brief history of gun control — see this article from the Poynter Institute. Among the many studies that look at the effectiveness of policies and programs to reduce gun violence, a 2012 metastudy in the journal *Crime & Delinquency* stands out for its comprehensiveness. The effectiveness of having guns in the home for self-defense is also an area of significant research.

What some researchers call "rampage violence" — such as the shootings in Newtown, Conn., at Columbine High and Virginia Tech, and at Rep. Gabrielle Giffords's political event in Tucson — plays a prominent role in the national consciousness, often touching off political debates over gun control laws, shifts in the culture and the role of violent media, particularly video games.

Though each act of violence has a distinct context, over the past decade the social science research community has continued to search for more general frameworks of understanding. But some researchers believe that establishing more precise psychological/criminal profiles in the hope of preventing such events through interventions may ultimately prove elusive. Though much speculation is offered in the media immediately afterward, scholars often note the limits of existing knowledge. (For a review of the research literature on such profiling, see the first article below.) It should be said that the connection between violence and severe mental illness is often over-simplified in the news media, and claims should be framed and informed by the existing empirical research. A 2013 survey and report published in *The New England Journal of Medicine* has data on the public's views on mental illness issues and violence, in the wake of the Newtown, Conn., school shooting incident.

In terms of violent acts in a school context, the FBI compiles useful background materials and data, as does the Centers for Disease Control.

Below are studies that provide an overview of the state of knowledge in this area:

"The Nature of Mass Murder and Autogenic Massacre"

Bowers, Thomas G.; Holmes, Eric S.; Rhom, Ashley. *Journal of Police and Criminal Psychology*, 2010, 25:59-66. doi: 10.1007/s11896-009-9059-6

Abstract: "Incidents of mass murder have gained considerable media attention, but are not well understood in behavioral sciences. Current definitions are weak, and may include politically or ideologically motivated phenomenon. Our current understanding of the phenomenon indicates these incidents are not peculiar to only western cultures, and appear to be increasing. Methods most prominently used include firearms by males who have experienced challenging setbacks in important social, familial and vocational domains. There often appears to be important autogenic components … including dysthymic reactions and similar antecedents. There have been observations of possible seasonal variations in mass murders, but research to date is inadequate to establish this relationship. It is recommended behavioral sciences and mental health researchers increase research efforts on understanding mass killings, as the current socioeconomic climate may increase vulnerability to this phenomenon, and the incidents are not well understood despite their notoriety."

"Rampage Violence Requires a New Type of Research"

Harris Jr., John M.; Harris, Robin B. *American Journal of Public Health*, June 2012, Vol. 102, No. 6, pp. 1054-1057. doi: 10.2105/ AJPH.2011.300545

Abstract: "Tragedies such as school shootings and the assault on Congresswoman Gabrielle Giffords share features that define them as acts of "rampage violence." These types of events can lead to despair about their inevitability and unpredictability. To understand and prevent rampage violence, we need to acknowledge that current discipline-based violence research is not well suited to this specific challenge. There are numerous important, unanswered research questions that can inform policies designed to prevent rampage violence. It is time to develop alternative research approaches to reduce the risk of rampage violence. Such approaches should incorporate transdisciplinary research models; flexible, outcomes-focused organizational structures similar to those used to investigate other catastrophic events; and an expanded inventory of analytic tools."

"The 'Pseudocommando' Mass Murderer: Part I, The Psychology of Revenge and Obliteration"

Knoll, James L. *Journal of American Academy of Psychiatry and the Law*, March 2010, 38:1:87-94

Abstract: "The pseudocommando is a type of mass murderer who kills in public during the daytime, plans his offense well in advance, and comes prepared with a powerful arsenal of weapons. He has no escape planned and expects to be killed during the incident. Research suggests that the pseudocommando is driven by strong feelings of anger and resentment, flowing from beliefs about being persecuted or grossly mistreated. He views himself as carrying out a highly personal agenda of payback. Some mass murderers take special steps to send a final communication to the public or news media; these communications, to date, have received little detailed analysis. An offender's use of language may reveal important data about his state of mind, motivation, and psychopathology. Part I of this article reviews the research on the pseudocommando, as well as the psychology of revenge, with special attention to revenge fantasies. It is argued that revenge fantasies become the last refuge for the pseudocommando's mortally wounded self-esteem and ultimately enable him to commit mass murder-suicide." (Also see Part II of the article.)

"Attributing Blame in Tragedy: Understanding Attitudes About the Causes of Three Mass Shootings"

Haider-Markel, Donald P.; Joslyn, Mark R. American Political Science Association, 2011 annual meeting paper. Accessed through Social Science Research Network.

Abstract: "Individuals develop causal stories about the world around them that explain events, behaviors, and conditions. These stories may attribute causes to controllable components, such as individual choice, or uncontrollable components, such as systematic forces in the environment. Here we employ motivated reasoning and attribution theory to understand causal attributions to the 2007 Virginia Tech shootings, the 2009 Fort Hood shootings, and the 2011 Tucson, Arizona shootings. We argue that causal attributions stem from individual reasoning that is primarily motivated by existing dispositions and accuracy motives. Both motivations are present for attributions about these mass shootings and we seek to understand their significance and whether dispositional motives condition accuracy drives. We are able to test several hypotheses using individual level survey data from several national surveys to explain attributions about the shootings. Our findings suggest a substantial partisan divide on the causes of the tragedies and considerable differences between the least and most educated respondents. However, our analyses also reveal that while education has virtually no influence on the attributions made by Republicans, it heightens the differences among Democrats. We discuss these findings for the public's understanding of these tragedies and more broadly for attribution research."

"Psychological Profiles of School Shooters: Positive Directions and One Big Wrong Turn"

Ferguson, Christopher J.; Coulson, Mark; Barnett, Jane. *Journal of Police Crisis Negotiations*, 2011, Vol. 11, Issue 2. doi: 10.1080/15332586.2011.581523

Abstract: "A wave of school shootings in the mid- to late 1990s led to great interest in attempts to 'profile' school shooters with an eye both on identifying imminent perpetrators and preventing further incidents. Given that school shootings are generally rare, and many perpetrators are killed during their crimes, the availability of school shooters for research is obviously limited. Not surprisingly, initial profiles of school shooters were arguably of limited value. Although school shooting incidents, particularly by minors, have declined, some evidence has emerged to elucidate the psychological elements of school shooting incidents. School shooting incidents may follow extreme versions of etiological pathways seen for less extreme youth violence, and youthful school shooters appear more similar than different to adult perpetrators of mass shootings. The quest to understanding school shootings has led to several wrong turns, most notably the quixotic desire by politicians, advocates, and some scholars to link both school shootings and less extreme youth violence to playing violent video games, despite considerable and increasing evidence to the contrary."

"The Autogenic (Self-Generated) Massacre"

Mullen, P.E. *Behavioral Sciences and the Law*, 2004, 22(3):311-23.

Abstract: "Mass killings can be of a variety of types including family slayings, cult killings, and the by-product of other criminal activities. This article focuses on massacres where the perpetrators indiscriminately kill people in pursuit of a highly personal agenda arising from their own specific social situation and psychopathology. Five cases are presented of this type of autogenic (self-generated) massacre, all of whom survived and were assessed by the author. Not only do these massacres follow an almost stereotypical course, but the perpetrators tend to share common social and psychological disabilities. They are isolates, often bullied in childhood, who have rarely established themselves in effective work roles as adults. They have personalities marked by suspiciousness, obsessional traits, and grandiosity. They often harbor persecutory beliefs, which may occasionally verge on the delusional. The autogenic massacre is essentially murder suicide, in which the perpetrators intend first to kill as many people as they can and then kill themselves. The script for this particular form of suicide has established itself in western society and is continuing to spread, and to diversify."

"Mass Murder: An Analysis of Extreme Violence"

Fox, James Alan; Levin, Jack. *Journal of Applied Psychoanalytic Studies.* Vol. 5, No. 1 (2003), 47-64, doi: 10.1023/A:1021051002020.

Findings: "Mass murder involves the slaughter of four or more victims by one or a few assailants within a single event, lasting but a few minutes or as long as several hours. More than just arbitrary, using this minimum body count — as opposed to a two- or three-victim threshold suggested by others (e.g., Ressler et al., 1988, Holmes and Holmes, 2001) — helps to distinguish multiple killing from homicide generally. Moreover, by restricting our attention to acts committed by one or a few offenders, our working definition of multiple homicide also excludes highly organized or institutionalized killings (e.g., war crimes and large-scale acts of political terrorism as well as certain acts of highly organized crime rings). Although state-sponsored killings are important in their own right, they may be better explained through the theories and methods of political science than criminology. Thus, for example, the definition of multiple homicide would include the crimes committed by Charles Manson and his followers, but not those of Hitler's Third Reich, or the 9/11 terrorists, despite some similarities in the operations of authority."

"Predicting the Risk of Future Dangerousness"

Phillipps, Robert T.M. *Virtual Mentor.* June 2012, Volume 14, Number 6: 472-476.

Abstract: "A consequence if not a driving force of the pendulum swing away from benevolence and toward the protection of others has been increased attention to an individual's dangerousness, with the operative presumption that dangerousness is often the result of a mental illness. But dangerousness is not always the result of mental illness. Individuals who commit violent or aggressive acts often do so for reasons unrelated to mental illness.... Research, in fact, confirms the error in associating dangerousness with mental illness, showing that 'the vast majority of people who are violent do not suffer from mental illnesses. The absolute risk of violence among the mentally ill as a group is still very small and ... only a small proportion of the violence in our society can be attributed to persons who are mentally ill.' Violence is not a diagnosis nor is it a disease. Potential to do harm is not a symptom or a sign of mental illness, rather it must be the central consideration when assessing future dangerousness."

"Predicting Dangerousness With Two Million Adolescent Clinical Inventory Psychopathy Scales: The Importance of Egocentric and Callous Traits"

Salekin, Randall, T.; Ziegler, Tracey A.; Larrea, Maria A.; Anthony, Virginia Lee; Bennett, Allyson D.
Journal of Personality Assessment, 2003, Vol. 80, Issue 2. doi: 10.1207/S15327752JPA8002_04.

Abstract: "Psychopathy in youth has received increased recognition as a critical clinical construct for the evaluation and management of adolescents who have come into contact with the law (e.g., Forth, Hare, & Hart, 1990; Frick, 1998; Lynam, 1996, 1998). Although considerable attention has been devoted to the adult construct of psychopathy and its relation to recidivism, psychopathy in adolescents has been less thoroughly researched. Recently, a psychopathy scale (Murrie and Cornell Psychopathy Scale; Murrie & Cornell, 2000) was developed from items of the Million Adolescent Clinical Inventory (MACI; Millon, 1993). This scale was found to be highly related to the Psychopathy Checklist-Revised (Hare, 1991) and was judged to have demonstrated good criterion validity. A necessary step in the validation process of any psychopathy scale is establishing its predictive validity. With this in mind, we investigated the ability of the MACI Psychopathy Scale to predict recidivism with 55 adolescent offenders 2 years after they had been evaluated at a juvenile court evaluation unit. In addition, we devised a psychopathy scale from MACI items that aligned more closely with Cooke and Michie (2001) and Frick, Bodin, and Barry's (2001) recommendations for the refinement of psychopathy and tested its predictive validity. Results indicate that both scales had predictive utility. Interpersonal and affective components of the revised scale were particularly important in the prediction of both general and violent reoffending."

"Violent Video Game Effects on Aggression, Empathy and Prosocial Behavior in Eastern and Western Countries: A Meta-Analytic Review"

Anderson, Craig A.; Shibuya, Akiko; Ihori, Nobuko; Swing, Edward L.; Bushman, Brad J.; Sakamoto, Akira; Rothstein, Hannah R.; Saleem, Muniba. *Psychological Bulletin*, March 2010, Vol. 136(2), 151-173

Abstract: "Meta-analytic procedures were used to test the effects of violent video games on aggressive behavior, aggressive cognition, aggressive affect, physiological arousal, empathy/desensitization, and prosocial behavior. Unique features of this meta-analytic review include (a) more restrictive methodological quality inclusion criteria than in past meta-analyses; (b) cross-cultural comparisons; (c) longitudinal studies for all outcomes except physiological arousal; (d) conservative statistical controls; (e) multiple moderator analyses; and (f) sensitivity analyses. Social-cognitive models and cultural differences between Japan and Western countries were used to generate theory-based predictions. Meta-analyses yielded significant effects for all 6 outcome variables. The pattern of results for different outcomes and research designs (experimental, cross-sectional, longitudinal) fit theoretical predictions well. The evidence strongly suggests that exposure to violent video games is a causal risk factor for increased aggressive behavior, aggressive cognition, and aggressive affect and for decreased empathy and prosocial behavior. Moderator analyses revealed significant research design effects, weak evidence of cultural differences in susceptibility and type of measurement effects, and no evidence of sex differences in susceptibility. Results of various sensitivity analyses revealed these effects to be robust, with little evidence of selection (publication) bias."

"'It's Better to Overreact': School Officials' Fear and Perceived Risk of Rampage Attacks and the Criminalization of American Public Schools"

Madfis, Eric. *Critical Criminology*, September 2015. doi: 10.1007/
s10612-015-9297-0.

Abstract: "In recent decades, highly-publicized school rampage attacks with multiple victims have caused widespread fear throughout the United States. Pulling from in-depth interviews with school officials (administrators, counselors, security and police officers, and teachers), this article discusses officials' perceptions of fear and risk regarding rampage shootings and how this relates to their justification for and acquiescence to the expansion of punitive discipline and increased security. Data collected in this study provide additional understanding of the causes of enhanced discipline and security from the perspective of those tasked with administering school safety in the wake of Columbine. Utilizing insight from moral panic theory, the findings suggest that, when the genuinely high potential cost of school massacres fused with an exaggerated perception of their likelihood and randomness, school rampage attacks came to be viewed as a risk that could not be tolerated and must be avoided at nearly any cost."

"Posttraumatic Stress Among Students after the Shootings at Virginia Tech"

Hughes, Michael; Brymer, Melissa; Chiu, Wai Tat; Fairbank, John A.;
Jones, Russell T.; Pynoos, Robert S.; Rothwell, Virginia; Steinberg,
Alan M.; Kessler, Ronald C. *Psychological Trauma: Theory,*

Research, Practice, and Policy, December 2011, Vol. 3(4), 403-411.
doi: 10.1037/a0024565

Abstract: "On April 16, 2007, in the worst campus shooting incident in U.S. history, 49 students and faculty at Virginia Polytechnic Institute and State University (Virginia Tech) were shot, of whom 32 were killed. A cross-sectional survey of 4,639 Virginia Tech students was carried out the following summer/fall to assess PTSD symptoms using the Trauma Screening Questionnaire (TSQ). High levels of posttraumatic stress symptoms (probable PTSD) were experienced by 15.4% of respondents 3 to 4 months following the shooting. Exposure to trauma-related stressors varied greatly, from 64.5% unable to confirm the safety of friends to 9.1% who had a close friend killed. Odds ratios for stressors predicting high levels of posttraumatic stress symptoms were highest for losses (2.6-3.6; injury/death of someone close) and inability to confirm the safety of friends (2.5). Stressor effects were unrelated to age, gender, and race/ethnicity. The exposures that explained most of the cases of high posttraumatic stress symptoms were inability to confirm the safety of friends (30.7%); death of a (not close) friend (20.3%); and death of a close friend (10.1%). The importance of high-prevalence low-impact stressors resulted in a low *concentration* of probable cases of PTSD, making it difficult to target a small, highly exposed segment of students for mental health treatment outreach. The high density of student social networks will likely make this low concentration of probable PTSD a common feature of future college mass trauma incidents, requiring broad-based outreach to find students needing mental health treatment interventions."

"Adjustment Following the Mass Shooting at Virginia Tech: The Roles of Resource Loss and Gain"

Littleton, Heather L.; Axsom, Danny; Grills-Taquechel, Amie E.

Psychological Trauma: Theory, Research, Practice and Policy, September 2009, Vol. 1(3), 206-219. doi: 10.1037/a0017468

Abstract: "Unfortunately, many individuals will be exposed to traumatic events during their lifetime. The experience of loss and gain of valued resources may represent important predictors of psychological distress following these experiences. The current study examined the extent to which loss and gain of interpersonal and intrapersonal resources (e.g., hope, intimacy) predicted psychological distress among college women following the mass shooting at Virginia Tech (VT). Participants were 193 college women from whom pre-event psychological distress and social support data had been obtained. These women completed surveys regarding their psychological distress, coping, and resource loss and gain 2- and 6-months after the VT shooting. Structural equation modeling supported that resource loss predicted greater psychological distress 6 months after the shooting whereas resource gain was weakly related to lower levels of psychological distress. The study also revealed that social support and psychological distress prior to the shooting predicted resource loss, and social support and active coping with the shooting predicted resource gain. Implications of the results for research examining the roles of resource loss and gain in posttrauma adjustment and the development of interventions following mass trauma are discussed."

"Murder by Numbers: Monetary Costs Imposed by a Sample of Homicide Offenders"

DeLisi, Matt; Kosloski, Anna; Sween, Molly; Hachmeister Emily; Moore Matt; Drury, Alan. *Journal of Forensic Psychiatry & Psychology*, 2010, Vol. 21, Issue 4. doi: 10.1080/14789940903564388.

Abstract: "Prior research on the monetary costs of criminal careers has neglected to focus on homicide offenders and tended to minimize the public costs associated with crime. Drawing on expanded monetization estimates produced by Cohen and Piquero, this study assessed the monetary costs for five crimes (murder, rape, armed robbery, aggravated assault, and burglary) imposed by a sample of ($n = 654$) convicted and incarcerated murderers. The average cost per murder exceeded $17.25 million and the average murderer in the current sample posed costs approaching $24 million. The most violent and prolific offenders *singly* produced costs greater than $150-160 million in terms of victim costs, criminal justice costs, lost offender productivity, and public willingness-to-pay costs."

"More Support for Gun Rights, Gay Marriage than in 2008, 2004"
Pew Research Center, April 2012

Findings: Opinions on gun rights have shifted significantly over time. In 2000, 66% of Americans said controlling gun ownership was more important than protecting gun rights, while just 29% said rights were more important. By 2012, 49% supported gun rights versus 45% favoring gun control. Support for gun ownership among both men and women has increased from 2008, with a 14 percentage point increase in support for gun rights for men and a 9 percentage point increase for women. Partisan division over gun control has also grown in recent years. Republican support for gun rights increased from 65% in 2009 to 72% in 2012, while Independent support for gun rights increased from 48% in 2009 to 55% in 2012.

"Firearms and Violence: A Critical Review"
Wellford C.F.; Pepper J.V.; Petrie C.V. National Research Council of the National Academies, 2004. Washington, DC: National Academies Press.

Findings: "Empirical research on firearms and violence has resulted in important findings that can inform policy decisions. In particular, a wealth of descriptive information exists about the prevalence of firearm-related injuries and deaths, about firearms markets, and about the relationships between rates of gun ownership and violence. Research has found, for example, that higher rates of household firearms ownership are associated with higher rates of gun suicide, that illegal diversions from legitimate commerce are important sources of crime guns and guns used in suicide, that firearms are used defensively many times per day, and that some types of targeted police interventions may effectively lower gun crime and violence. This information is a vital starting point for any constructive dialogue about how to address the problem of firearms and violence. While much has been learned, much remains to be done, and this report necessarily focuses on the important unknowns in this field of study. The committee found that answers to some of the most pressing questions cannot be addressed with existing data and research methods, however well designed. For example, despite a large body of research, the committee found no credible evidence that the passage of right-to-carry laws decreases or increases violent crime, and there is almost no empirical evidence that the more than 80 prevention programs focused on gun-related violence have had any effect on children's behavior, knowledge, attitudes or beliefs about firearms. The committee found that the data available on these questions are too weak to support unambiguous conclusions or strong policy statements."

14

We Should Be More Skeptical About Gun Control

David B. Kopel

David B. Kopel is an American author, attorney, political science researcher, gun rights advocate, and contributing editor to several publications.

The main pillars of current gun restrictions are background checks, bans on assault weapons, and bans on high capacity ammunition magazines. Gun rights advocates can find numerous problems with each of these proposals. For example, background checks only cover purchases, but do not cover acquisitions of firearms from family members. Background checks are also rife with clerical errors. Basing gun bans on cosmetic features doesn't work. Most gun control advocates agree with gun rights extremists that some individuals will commit violent crimes, regardless of laws. But should this prevent us from even trying to stop them?

Introduction

Following news reports of the horrific murders on June 17, 2015, at the Emanuel African Methodist Episcopal Church in South Carolina, President Obama said Congress was partly to blame because it had not approved his gun-control proposals. "Once again," Obama said, "innocent people were killed in part because someone who wanted to inflict harm had no trouble getting their hands on a gun."[1] Obama added, "It is in our power to do something

"The Costs and Consequences of Gun Control," by David B. Kopel, The Cato Institute, 2015. Reprinted by permission © The Cato Institute, 2015.

about it. I say that recognizing the politics in this town foreclose a lot of avenues right now. But it would be wrong for us not to acknowledge [the politics]. At some point it's going to be important for the American people to come to grips with it."[2]

It is unfortunate that Obama chose to disparage those who disagree with him for their supposed fixation on grubby "politics" and indifference to murder victims. Whether Obama realizes it or not, there are good reasons to be skeptical of gun-control policies. This paper will scrutinize the three most common gun-control ideas that have been put forward in recent years: universal background checks, a ban on high-capacity magazines, and a ban on assault weapons. These proposals are misguided and will not prevent the crimes that typically prompt officials to make pleas for more gun control. Policymakers can take some steps to incapacitate certain mentally ill persons who are potentially violent. Yet, it would be wrong not to acknowledge that gun laws often cannot stop a person bent on murder. Policymakers should not pretend otherwise.

Universal Background Checks

Under current law, persons who are in the business of selling firearms must perform a criminal background check prior to any sale. After the Charleston shooting, some gun-control advocates want to expand the background check system further — so that it would cover occasional private sales as well. In July 2015, community leaders from Charleston appeared at a press conference on Capitol Hill with Dan Gross, president of the Brady Campaign to Prevent Gun Violence. They demanded that Congress vote on a bill to expand background checks.[3] And in a speech to the U.S. Conference of Mayors, presidential aspirant Hillary Clinton said it made no sense that Congress had failed to pass common-sense gun control, such as universal background checks.[4]

Dylann Roof, the racist who attacked the churchgoers in Charleston, had previously been arrested, and he had admitted to law enforcement officers that he was a user of methamphetamine. That was sufficient, under the federal Gun Control Act of 1968, to prohibit him from owning guns, because the statute bans gun ownership by illegal drug users. However, as the FBI later admitted, the bureau failed to properly enter into its database the prohibiting information that had been provided by local law enforcement.[5] This incident points to a key limitation to the background-check concept: bureaucratic errors. In 2013, the FBI conducted more than 21 million background checks for firearm purchases.[6] Given the massive scale of the system, there are always going to be errors as those records get misplaced or neglected.

Three other shootings in 2015 that garnered media attention show the limitations of background checks. Muhammad Youssef Abdulazeez attacked two military installations in Chattanooga, Tennessee on July 16. Like the Boston marathon bombers, Abdulazeez was a radicalized jihadi. He apparently radicalized after visiting his Palestinian relatives in Jordan. Abdulazeez was a U.S. citizen and purchased firearms lawfully after passing background checks. Professor James Alan Fox of Northeastern University, who studies mass shootings, explains that "mass killers are determined, deliberate and dead-set on murder. They plan methodically to execute their victims, finding the means no matter what laws or other impediments the state attempts to place in their way. To them, the will to kill cannot be denied."[7]

On July 23, John Russell Houser murdered several people in a movie theater in Lafayette, Louisiana. Houser was severely mentally ill; in 2008, a Georgia judge issued an order to apprehend him so that he could be held for five days for a mental health evaluation. The mental hospital records have not been released, but the hospital apparently did not petition for a longer involuntary commitment.[8] Had Houser been involuntarily committed, he would have become a prohibited person under the 1968 Gun Control Act.[9] But he was not, and so he passed a background check and purchased a handgun from a gun store in February 2014.[10] Houser shot 11 people, killing two, and then committed suicide when police arrived.[11] A background-check system cannot stop people like Houser, who are dangerous, yet have fallen through the cracks in the system and have no disqualifying record.

Christopher Harper-Mercer, who murdered nine people at Umpqua Community College in Roseburg, Oregon, on October 1, 2015, was not affected by one of the most severe background check statutes in the United States. The Oregon background-check law applies to almost all private firearm sales, not just commercial sales.[12] Despite this universal background check regime, all of the firearms recovered from the killer were legally purchased, either by him or his mother.[13] Harper-Mercer appears to have been seriously mentally ill, but neither he nor his mother were in any way impeded by background check laws.

Gun-control advocates often claim that 40 percent of annual firearms sales take place today without background checks. The *Washington Post* "fact-checker" has debunked that claim, giving it "Three Pinocchios."[14] The *Post* noted that the survey data used for the study on which the 40 percent claim is based are more than two decades old, which means they were collected prior to the National Instant Criminal Background Check System becoming operational in 1998. The survey only polled 251 people, and, upon asking whether their gun transfer involved a federally licensed dealer — that is, a federal firearms licensee (FFL) — gave respondents the choice of saying "probably" or "probably not" in addition to "yes" and "no."

From that survey, the report concluded that 35.7 percent of acquisitions did not involve a background check. But "acquisitions" is a much broader category than "purchases," which is the term used by advocates for gun control. Gifts and inheritances between family members or among close friends are acquisitions, but not purchases. When the *Post* asked researchers to correct for that distinction, the percentage of firearms purchased without a background check fell to between 14 and 22 percent. The *Post* subsequently conducted its own survey of Maryland residents, and found that 21 percent of respondents reported not having gone through a background check to purchase a firearm in the previous decade.

Even that 21 percent, which entails transactions between private, noncommercial sellers, is regulated by the federal law against giving a firearm to someone the transferor knows, or reasonably should know, is among the nine categories of prohibited persons under federal law (e.g., mentally impaired; convicted felons).[15] The assertion that nearly half of the gun sales in America are unregulated is simply false. Federal law governs as many gun sales and transfers as is practically enforceable already.

As a 2013 National Institute of Justice memo from Greg Ridgeway, acting director of the National Institute of Justice, acknowledged, a system requiring background checks for gun sales by non-FFLs is utterly unenforceable without a system of universal gun registration.[16] For FFLs, enforcement of record-keeping is routine. They are required to keep records of every gun which enters or leaves their inventory.[17] As regulated businesses, the vast majority of them will comply with whatever procedures are required for gun sales. Even the small minority of FFLs who might wish to evade the law have little practical opportunity to do so. Federal firearms licensees are subject to annual warrantless inspections for records review and to unlimited warrantless inspections in conjunction with a bona fide criminal investigation or when tracing a gun involved in a criminal investigation.[18] The wholesalers and manufacturers who supply the FFLs with guns must keep similar records, so a FFL who tried to keep a gun off the books would know that the very same gun would be in the wholesaler's records, with precise information about when the gun was shipped to the retailer.[19]

In contrast, if a rancher sells his own gun to a neighbor, there is no practical way to force the rancher and the neighbor to drive an hour into town, and then attempt to find a FFL who will run a background check for them, even though they are not customers of the FFL. Once the rancher has sold the gun to the neighbor, there is no practical way to prove that the neighbor acquired the gun after the date when the private sales background check came into effect. As the National Institute of Justice recognized, the only way to enforce the background-check law would be to require the retroactive registration of all currently owned firearms in the United States. Such a policy did not work in Canada, and anyone who thinks that Americans would be more willing to register their guns than Canadians is badly mistaken.[20]

In *Printz v. United States* (1997), Justice Clarence Thomas suggested that a mandatory federal check on "purely intrastate sale or possession of firearms" might violate the Second Amendment.[21] That view is supported by the Supreme Court's 2008 ruling in *District of Columbia v. Heller*. In *Heller*, the Court provided a list of "long-standing laws" that were "presumptively lawful" gun controls.[22] The inclusion of each item on the list, as an exception to the right to keep and bear arms, provides guidance about the scope of the right itself.

For example, the Court affirmed "prohibitions on the possession of firearms by felons and the mentally ill." Felons and the mentally ill are exceptions to the general rule that individual Americans have a right to possess arms. The exception only makes sense if the general rule stands. After all, if no one has a right to possess arms, then there is no need for a special rule that felons and the mentally ill may be barred from possessing arms.

The second exception to the right to keep and bear arms concerns "laws forbidding the carrying of firearms in sensitive places such as schools and government buildings." This exception proves another rule: Americans have a general right to carry firearms. If the Second Amendment only applied to the keeping of arms at home, and not to the bearing of arms in public places, then there would be no need to specify an exception for carrying arms in "sensitive places."

The third *Heller* exception concerns "laws imposing conditions and qualifications on the commercial sale of arms." Again, the exception proves the rule. The Second Amendment allows "conditions and qualifications" on the commercial sale of arms.

The Second Amendment does not presumptively allow Congress to impose "conditions and qualifications" on noncommercial transactions. At least *Heller* seems to suggest so.

Federal law has long defined what constitutes commercial sale of arms. A person is required to obtain a federal firearms license (and become subject to many conditions and qualifications when selling arms) if the person is engaged in the business of selling firearms. That means:

> a person who devotes time, attention, and labor to dealing in firearms as a regular course of trade or business with the principal objective of livelihood and profit through the repetitive purchase and resale of firearms, but such term shall not include a person who makes occasional sales, exchanges, or purchases of firearms for the enhancement of a personal collection or for a hobby, or who sells all or part of his personal collection of firearms.[23]

A person who is "engaged in the business, but who does not have an FFL, is guilty of a felony every time he sells a firearm.[24] Currently, the federal National Instant Criminal Background Check System law generally matches the constitutional standard set forth in *Heller*. It applies to all sales by persons who are engaged in the business (FFLs) and does not apply to transfers by persons who are not engaged in the business.[25]

After the 2012 Sandy Hook murders, Obama ordered the Bureau of Alcohol, Tobacco, Firearms and Explosives (ATF) to inform FFLs about how they can perform a background check for private persons who would like such a check.[26] On a voluntary basis, that order was legitimate, but it would be constitutionally dubious to mandate it.

As a practical matter, criminals who are selling guns to each other (which is illegal and subject to severe mandatory sentencing) are not going to comply with a background-check mandate.[27] It would be irrelevant to them. Ordinary law-abiding citizens who sell guns to each other might be willing to take the gun to a firearm store for a voluntary check, provided that the check is not subject to a special fee, that there is no registration, and that the check is convenient and expeditious. The new ATF regulations for private-party sales comply with two of those three conditions; however, the regulations do require that dealers keep permanent records on the buyer and one of the make, model, and serial number of the gun, just as if the dealer were selling a firearm out of his own inventory. The dealer-based system of registration, created by the Gun Control Act of 1968, avoids the dangers of a central registry of guns, but it does have risks: a government that wanted to confiscate guns could simply harvest the dealer sales records.

Proposals concerning universal background checks have fairly strong support in public opinion polls, but those polls are premised on the idea that the check would be applied to the actual sale of firearms. To the contrary, in proposed legislation, the requirement for government authorization (via a background check and paperwork identical to buying a gun) would apply to far more than gun sales. The proposals apply to all firearms "transfers."[28] A "transfer" might be showing a new gun to a friend and letting him handle the gun for a few minutes.

For example, Senate bill S.649 (2013), introduced by Sen. Harry Reid (D-NV), goes far beyond controlling the actual sale of firearms. Consider a case in which a woman buys a common revolver at age 25, and keeps it her entire life. She never sells the gun. But over her lifetime, she may engage in dozens of firearms transfers:

- The woman loans the gun to her sister, who takes it on a camping trip for the weekend.
- While the woman is out of town on a business trip for two weeks, she gives the gun to her brother.
- If the woman lives on a farm, she allows all of her relatives on the farm to take the gun into the fields for pest and predator control.
- If the woman is in the Army Reserve, and she is called up for an overseas deployment, she gives the gun to her brother-in-law for temporary safe-keeping. When she goes out of

town on vacation every year, she also temporarily gives her gun to her brother-in-law.

- One time, when a neighbor is being threatened by an abusive ex-boyfriend who is a stalker, the woman lets the neighbor borrow the gun for several days, until the neighbor can buy her own gun.
- If the woman becomes a firearms safety instructor, she may teach classes at office parks, school buildings, or gun stores. Following the standard curriculum of gun safety classes, such as those required by the National Rifle Association, the woman will bring some unloaded guns to a classroom, and under her supervision, students will learn the first steps in handling the gun, including how to load and unload the gun (using inert dummy ammunition). During the class, the firearms will be transferred dozens of times, as students practice how to hand a gun to someone safely.

Under S. 649, every one of the above activities would be a felony, punished the same as if the woman had knowingly sold the firearm to a convicted violent felon. Here is the pertinent provision: "It shall be unlawful for any person who is not licensed under this chapter to transfer a firearm to any other person who is not licensed under this chapter."[29]

This is not "gun control" in the constitutionally legitimate sense — reasonable laws that protect public safety without interfering with the responsible ownership and use of firearms. To the contrary, such grotesquely overbroad laws have the effect of turning almost every gun owner into a felon by outlawing the ordinary, innocent, and safety-enhancing ways in which firearms in the United States are "transferred" millions of times every year.

While S. 649 has a few exceptions to the ban on transfers, not one of them apply to the situations described above:

- One can make a "bona-fide gift" (but not a three-hour loan) to certain close family members, not including aunts, uncles, nieces, nephews, in-laws, or civil union partners.

- One can let someone else borrow a gun for up to seven days, but only within the curtilage of one's house. Not on the open space one owns, and even a spouse cannot borrow a gun for eight days.
- One can leave a firearm to another in a written will. But on one's deathbed, it would be unlawful to leave a gun to one's best friend.
- One can share a gun at a shooting range (but only if the shooting range is owned by a corporation, not on public lands, and not at a shooting range on one's own property).
- One can share a gun at a shooting match, but only if the match is operated by a non-profit corporation or the government — not a match organized by the National Rifle Association, and not a match organized by a firearms manufacturer.
- One can share a gun while out hunting in the field, but back at the hunting camp, it would be illegal to clean someone else's gun.[30]

Even if there was no Second Amendment, the arbitrary rules of the various exemptions would make Senator Reid's bill of very dubious constitutionality. As interpreted by the courts, due process requires that all laws have a legitimate purpose and at least a rational connection to that purpose.[31]

High-Capacity Magazines

Another gun-control initiative that has been recently revived is the idea to ban high-capacity magazines. The Los Angeles City Council, for example, passed an ordinance that would prohibit city residents from possessing handgun or rifle magazines that hold more than 10 rounds of ammunition.[32] The New York state legislature enacted a similar ban in 2013.[33] Such bans are unconstitutional and undermine public safety.

A magazine is the part of the firearm where the ammunition is stored. Sometimes the magazine is part of the firearm itself, as in tube magazines underneath barrels. This is the norm for shotguns. For many rifles, and almost all handguns that use magazines, the magazine is detachable. A detachable magazine is a rectangular or curved box, made of metal or plastic. At the bottom of the box is a spring, which pushes a new round of ammunition into the firing chamber after the empty shell from the previous round has been ejected. [34] The caliber of the gun does not determine what size magazine can be used. Any gun that uses a detachable magazine can accommodate a detachable magazine of any size. So, for example, a gun with a detachable magazine holding 10 rounds can also accommodate a magazine that holds 20 rounds.

The 1994 federal ban on assault weapons included a ban on large magazines. As indicated by the bill's title (the Public Safety and Recreational Firearms Use Protection Act), that ban was predicated on the idea that recreational firearm use is legitimate, but other firearms use is not.[35] Yet for target-shooting competitions, there are many events that use magazines holding more than 10 rounds. For hunting, about half the states limit the magazine size that a hunter may carry in the field, but half do not. In some scenarios, such as deer hunting, a hunter will rarely get off more than two shots at a particular animal. In other situations, particularly pest control, the use of 11- to 30-round magazines is typical because the hunter will be firing multiple shots. Such pests include the hunting of packs of feral hogs and wild animals, such as prairie dogs and coyotes.

More generally, the rifle that might be used to shoot only one or two rounds at a deer might be needed for self-defense against a bear or against a criminal attack. In 2012, Arizona repealed its limitations on magazine capacity for hunters precisely because of the possible need for self-defense against unexpected encounters with cartel gangs in the southern part of the state.[36] In that region, it is well known that drug traffickers and human traffickers use the same wild and lonely lands that hunters do.

For the firearms that are most often chosen for self-defense, the claim that any magazine holding more than 10 (or 7) rounds is "high capacity" or "large" is incorrect. The term "high-capacity magazine" might have a legitimate meaning when it refers to a magazine that extends far beyond that intended for the gun's optimal operation. For example, although a semiautomatic handgun can accept a 40-round magazine, such a magazine typically extends far beneath the gun grip, and it is therefore impractical to use with a concealed-carry permit. For most handguns, a 40-round magazine could be called "high-capacity."

The persons who have the most need for actual high-capacity magazines are those who would have great difficulty changing a magazine — such as elderly persons or persons with disabilities. For an able-bodied person, changing a magazine only takes a few seconds. Typically a gun's magazine-release button is near the trigger. To change a magazine, the person holding the gun presses the magazine-release button with a thumb or finger. The magazine instantly drops to the floor. While one hand was pushing the magazine-release button, the other hand can grab a fresh magazine (which might be carried in a special holster on a belt) and bring it toward the gun. The moment the old magazine drops out, a fresh one is inserted.[37]

Although one can quickly change magazines, persons being attacked by criminals will typically prefer not to spend even a few seconds for a magazine change. The stress of being attacked usually impedes fine motor skills, making it much more difficult to insert the magazine.[38] That is why many semiautomatic handguns come factory-standard with a magazine of 11 to 20 rounds. Thus, a ban on magazines with a capacity of more than 10 rounds means a ban on some of the most common and most useful magazines purchased for purposes of recreational target practice and self-defense.

Why might someone need a factory-standard 17-round magazine for a common 9mm handgun? As noted, standard-capacity magazines can be very useful for self-defense. This is especially true if a defender faces multiple attackers, an attacker is wearing heavy clothing or body armor, an attacker who is turbo-charged by methamphetamine or cocaine, or an attacker who poses an active threat from behind cover. In stressful circumstances, police as well as civilians often miss when firing a handgun even at close range, so having the extra rounds can be crucial.

It is important to consider the advantages a criminal has over his intended victims. The criminal has the element of surprise, whereas the victim is the one surprised. The criminal can decide at leisure what weaponry he will bring; whereas the victim must respond with what's at hand at the moment of attack. A criminal can bring several guns, or lots of magazines; whereas the victim will usually have on hand, at most, a single defensive gun with only as much ammunition as is in that gun. Thus, legislation confining law-abiding victims to magazines of 10 or fewer magnifies the criminal's advantage over his intended victim.

One fact that proves the usefulness of standard-capacity magazines is that most police officers use them. An officer typically carries a semiautomatic handgun on a belt holster as his primary sidearm. The magazine capacity is usually in the 11 to 20 range. Likewise, the long gun carried in police patrol cars is quite often an AR-15 rifle with a 30-round magazine.[39]

Violent confrontations are unpredictable; for example, if a person is fighting against one or two perpetrators, he may not know if there is an additional, hidden attacker. Thus, defensive gun users need to keep a reserve of ammunition. So even though armed defenders do not usually fire more than 10 shots, reducing reserve capacity (e.g., from a standard 17-round magazine to a 10-round substitute) will reduce the number of defensive shots. Fewer shots fired at the attacker reduces the risk of injury to the attacker, and thereby raises the risk of injury to the victim.

Would a Magazine Ban Be Beneficial?

The National Institute of Justice study found that the 1994-2004 federal ban on the manufacture of large magazines had no discernible benefit because the existing supply of such magazines was so vast.[40]

The types of criminals most likely to get into shootouts with the police or with other criminals are precisely those who are very aware of what is available on the black market. Although gun prohibitionists often link assault weapons to gang violence associated with the illegal drug trade, they miss the irony of their argument.[41] They are, in effect, claiming that the very gangs operating the black market in drugs will somehow be restricted from acquiring high-capacity magazines by legislation limiting the manufacture and sale of such magazines. The claim — at least as it pertains to career criminals — is ludicrous. If gangsters can obtain all the cocaine they want, despite a century of prohibition, they will be able to obtain 15-round magazines.

What about the typical perpetrators of random mass attacks — mentally ill young men? They, too, could acquire magazines by theft, or on the black market. Given that 36 percent of American high school seniors illegally acquire and consume marijuana, it is clear that plenty of people who are not gangsters or career criminals use the black market.[42] Besides that, the truly high-capacity magazines, such as a 100-round drum, are very prone to malfunction. For example, during the 2012 mass murder at the movie theater in Aurora, Colorado, the murderer's 100-round magazine jammed, allowing people to escape.[43] Hundred-round magazines are novelty items and are not standard for self-defense by civilians or police.

Advocates of a ban on standard-capacity magazines assert that while the attacker is changing the magazine, an intended victim might be able to subdue him — yet they cannot point to a single instance where this actually happened. They cite a trilogy of events that happened in Tucson, Arizona (2011), Aurora, Colorado (2012), and Newtown, Connecticut (2013). In fact, all of those events involved gun jams, not magazine changes. At Newtown, the criminal changed magazines seven times and no one escaped, but when his rifle jammed, people did escape. Clearing a gun jam takes much longer than changing a magazine. Fixing a gun jam involves all the steps of a magazine change (remove the empty magazine and insert a new one) plus all the intermediate steps of doing whatever is necessary to fix the jam. Similarly, in the Luby's cafeteria murders (24 dead), the perpetrator replaced magazines multiple times. In the Virginia Tech murders (32 dead), the perpetrator changed magazines 17 times.[44]

Advocates of banning magazines larger than 10 rounds call them "high capacity." Again, this is incorrect. The standard manufacturer-supplied magazines for many handguns have capacities up to 20 rounds; for rifles, standard magazine capacity is up to 30. This has been true for decades. Indeed, magazines holding more than 10 rounds constitute 47 percent of all magazines sold in the United States in the last quarter century.[45] There are tens of millions of such magazines. A law that was really about high-capacity magazines would cover the after-market magazines of 75 or 100 rounds, which have minuscule market share, and which are not standard for any firearm. As of 2011, there were approximately 332 million firearms in the United States not in military hands.[46] With the rough estimate that one-third of guns are handguns, most gun owners owning at least two magazines per gun, and 47 percent of magazines holding more than 10 rounds, the number of large magazines in the United States is at least in the tens of millions. When one also takes into account rifle magazines, the number of American magazines holding more than 10 rounds could be more than 100 million. That in itself is sufficient, according to the Supreme Court's *Heller* precedent, to make the ban unconstitutional.

Assault Weapons

Gun-control advocates have been calling for a ban on "assault weapons" for more than 25 years, especially in the aftermath of a notorious crime, regardless of the facts. For example, the Charleston criminal used an ordinary handgun. Yet South Carolina state senator Marlon Kimpson immediately proposed a statewide ban on assault weapons.[47] Democratic presidential hopeful Martin O'Malley told his supporters that the Charleston crime was proof of a "national crisis" and that tougher gun laws were needed at the federal level, including a new ban on assault weapons.[48]

Before examining the details of a ban, it should be noted at the outset that the term "assault weapons" is a political gimmick designed to foster confusion. The so-called "assault weapons" are not machine guns. They do not fire automatically. They fire only one bullet each time the trigger is pressed, just like every other ordinary firearm. They are not more powerful than other firearms. To the contrary, their ammunition is typically intermediate in power, less powerful than ammunition that is made for big-game hunting.

The Difference Between Automatic and Semiautomatic

For an automatic firearm, commonly called a machine gun, if the shooter presses the trigger and holds it, the gun will fire continuously, automatically, until the ammunition runs out.[49] Ever since the National Firearms Act of 1934, automatics have been heavily regulated by federal law. Anyone who wishes to acquire one must pay a $200 federal transfer tax, must be fingerprinted and photographed, and must complete a months-long registration process with the ATF. In addition, the transferee must be granted written permission by local law enforcement. Once registered, the gun may not be taken out of state without advance written permission from the ATF.[50] Since 1986, the manufacture of new automatics for sale to persons other than government agents has been forbidden by federal law.[51] Automatics in the United States have never been common; today the least expensive ones cost nearly ten thousand dollars.[52]

The automatic firearm was invented in 1884 by Hiram Maxim. The early Maxim guns were heavy and bulky and required a two-man crew to operate.[53] In 1943, a new type of automatic was invented, the "assault rifle." The assault rifle is light enough for a soldier to carry for long periods of time. Soon, the assault rifle became a very common infantry weapon. Some examples include the U.S. Army M-16, the Soviet AK-47, and the Swiss militia SIG SG 550. The AK-47 can be found throughout the Third World, but there are only a few hundred in the United States, mostly belonging to firearms museums and wealthy collectors.

The definition of "assault rifle" is supplied by the Defense Intelligence Agency: "short, compact, selective-fire weapons that fire a cartridge intermediate in power between a submachine gun and rifle cartridges."[54] If you use the term "assault rifle," persons who are knowledgeable about firearms will know precisely what kinds of guns you are referring to. The definition of assault rifle has never changed because the definition describes particular objects in the real world — just like the definitions of "table" or "umbrella." In contrast, the definition of "assault weapon" has never been stable. The phrase is an epithet. It has been applied to double-barreled shotguns, to single-shot guns (guns whose ammunition capacity is only a single round), and to many other ordinary handguns, shotguns, and rifles.

The first assault-weapon ban was in California in 1989. It was created by legislative staffers who thumbed through a picture book of guns and decided which guns looked bad.[55] The result was an incoherent law which, among other things, outlawed certain firearms that do not exist since the staffers just copied the typographical errors from the book or associated a model by one manufacturer with another manufacturer whose name happened to appear on the same page.[56]

Over the last quarter century, the definition kept shifting. The only consistency in what is dubbed an assault weapon seems to be how much gun prohibitionists believe they can outlaw given the political circumstances of the moment. One recent version is Sen. Dianne Feinstein's (D-CA) bill introduced after the Sandy Hook murders; it bans more than 120 types of guns by name, and hundreds more by generic definitions.[57] Another is the pair of bills defeated in the January 2013 lame-duck session of the Illinois legislature, which would have outlawed most handguns by dubbing them assault weapons.[58] In Colorado, the legislature rejected a bill in 2013 that would have classified as assault weapons guns such as an old-fashioned double-barreled shotgun, or single shot rifles and shotguns, which can only hold one round of ammunition.[59]

While the definitions of what to ban keep changing, a few things remain consistent: the definitions do not cover automatic firearms, such as genuine assault rifles. The definitions do not ban guns based on how fast they fire or how powerful they are. Instead, the definitions are based on the name of a gun, or on whether a firearm has certain accessories or components, such as a bayonet lug, or a grip in the "wrong" place. Most, but not all, of the guns which have been labeled assault weapons are semiautomatics. Many people who are unfamiliar with firearms think that a gun that is semiautomatic must be essentially the same as an automatic. That is incorrect.

Semiautomatic firearms were invented in the 1890s and have been common in the United States ever since. Today, 82 percent of new American handguns are semiautomatics. A large share of rifles and shotguns are also semiautomatics.[60] Among the most popular semiautomatic firearms are the Colt 1911 pistol (named for the year it was invented, and still considered one of the best self-defense handguns); the Ruger 10/22 rifle (which fires the low-powered .22 Long Rifle cartridge, popular for small-game hunting or for target shooting at distances less than a hundred yards); the Remington 1100 shotgun (very popular for bird hunting and home defense); and the AR-15 rifle (popular for hunting game no larger than deer, for target shooting, and for home defense). All of these guns were invented in the mid-1960s or earlier. All of them have, at various times, been characterized as assault weapons.

Unlike an automatic firearm, a semiautomatic fires only one round of ammunition when the trigger is pressed. (A "round" is one unit of ammunition. For a rifle or handgun, a round has one bullet. For a shotgun, a single round contains multiple pellets of shot.) In some other countries, a semiautomatic is usually called a "self-loading" gun. This accurately describes what makes the gun "semi"-automatic. When the gun is fired, the projectile travels from the firing chamber, down the barrel, and out the muzzle. Left behind in the firing chamber is the now-empty case or shell that contained the bullet (or shot) and the gunpowder. In a semiautomatic, some of the energy from firing is used to eject the empty shell and load a fresh round of ammunition into the firing chamber. The gun is then ready to shoot again — when the user is ready to press the trigger.

In some other types of firearms, the user must perform some action in order to eject the empty shell and load the next round. This could be moving a bolt back and forth (bolt-action rifles); moving a lever down and then up (lever-action rifles); or pulling and then pushing a pump or slide (pump-action and slide-action rifles and shotguns). A revolver (the second-most popular type of handgun) does not require the user to take any additional action in order to fire the next round.[61]

The semiautomatic has two principle advantages over lever-action, bolt-action, slide-action, and pump-action guns. First, many hunters prefer it because the semiautomatic mechanism allows a faster second shot. The difference may be less than a second, but for a hunter, that can make all the difference. Second, the semiautomatic's use of gunpowder energy to eject the empty case and to load the next round substantially reduces how much recoil is felt by the shooter. This makes the gun much more comfortable to shoot, especially for beginners, or for persons without substantial upper-body strength. The reduced recoil makes the gun easier to keep on target for the next shot, which is important for hunting and target shooting, and very important for self-defense.

Semiautomatics also have a disadvantage. They are more prone to mechanical jams than are simpler, older types of firearms, such as revolvers. Contrary to the hype of anti-gun advocates and less-responsible journalists, there is no rate-of-fire difference between a so-called assault semiautomatic gun and any other semiautomatic gun.

Are Semiautomatics More Powerful Than Other Guns?

The power of a firearm is measured by the kinetic energy it delivers. Kinetic energy is based on the mass of the projectile and its velocity.[62] So, a heavier bullet will have more kinetic energy than a lighter one moving at the same speed. A faster bullet will have more kinetic energy than a slower bullet of the same weight.[63] How much kinetic energy a gun delivers has nothing to do with whether it is a semiautomatic, a lever action, a bolt action, or a revolver. What matters is the weight of the bullet, how much gunpowder is in the particular round of ammunition, and the length of the barrel.[64] None of this has anything to do with whether the gun is a semiautomatic.

With respect to the rifles that some people call "assault weapons," semiautomatic rifles tend to be intermediate in power as far as rifles go. Consider the AR-15 rifle, a variant of the military's M-16, in its most common caliber, the .223. The bullet is only slightly wider than the puny .22 bullet, but it is longer and heavier. Using typical ammunition, an AR-15 in .223 would have 1,395 foot-pounds of kinetic energy.[65] That is more than a tiny rifle cartridge such as the .17 Remington, which might carry 801 foot-pounds of kinetic energy. In contrast, a big-game cartridge, like the .444 Marlin, might have 3,040 foot-pounds of kinetic energy.[66] That is why rifles like the AR-15 in their most common calibers are suitable, and often used, for hunting small to medium animals, such as rabbits or deer, but are not suitable for big game, such as elk or moose.[67]

Many of the ever-changing group of guns which are labeled assault weapons use detachable magazines (a box with an internal spring) to hold their ammunition. This is a characteristic shared by many other firearms, including many non-semiautomatic rifles (particularly bolt actions), and by the large majority of handguns. Whatever the merits of restricting magazine size (discussed above), the ammunition capacity of a firearm depends on the size of the detachable magazine. If one wants to control magazine size, there is no point in banning certain guns that can use detachable magazines, while not banning other guns that also use detachable magazines.

Bans by Name

Rather than banning guns based on rate of fire, or firepower, the various legislative attempts to define an assault weapon have taken two approaches: banning guns by name and banning guns according to certain features.

After a quarter century of legislative attempts to define assault weapon, the flagship bill for prohibitionists, drafted by Senator Feinstein, still relies on banning more than 120 guns by name. That in itself demonstrates that assault weapons prohibitions are not about guns that are more dangerous than other guns. After all, if a named gun really has physical characteristics that make it more dangerous than other guns, then legislators ought to be able to describe those characteristics and ban guns (regardless of name) that have those supposedly dangerous characteristics.

Bans by Features

An alternative approach to defining assault weapon has been to prohibit guns that have one or more items from a list of features. The problem here is that the listed features have nothing to do with a gun's rate of fire, its ammunition capacity, or its firepower. Here are some of the various items that Senator Feinstein finds objectionable:

Bayonet lugs. A bayonet lug gives a gun a military appearance, but it has nothing to do with criminal activity. Drive-by bayonetings are not a problem in this country.

Attachments for rocket launchers and grenade launchers. Since nobody makes guns for the civilian market that have such features, these bans would affect nothing.[68]

Folding or telescoping stocks. Telescoping stocks on long guns are very popular because they allow shooters to adjust the gun to their own size and build, to different types of clothing, or to their shooting position. Folding stocks also make a rifle or shotgun much easier to carry in a backpack while hunting or camping. Even with a folding stock, the long gun is still far larger, and less concealable, than a handgun.

Grips. The Feinstein bill outlaws any long gun that has a grip, or anything which can function as a grip. In the Rambo movie series, Sylvester Stallone would spray fire from his hip with an automatic rifle, which had a pistol grip. In real life, a grip helps a responsible shooter stabilize a semiautomatic or other rifle while holding the stock against his shoulder. It is particularly useful in hunting where the shooter will not have sandbags or a benchrest, or perhaps anything else, on which to rest the forward part of the rifle. Accurate hunting is humane hunting. And should a long gun be needed for self-defense, accuracy can save the victim's life.

Some gun-control advocates seem to oppose firearms accuracy. On the *PBS Newshour*, Josh Horwitz, an employee of the Coalition to Stop Gun Violence, said that grips should be banned because they prevent "muzzle rise" and thereby allow the shooter to stay on target.[69] Well, yes, a grip does help stabilize the gun so that a second shot (whether at a deer or a violent attacker) will go where the first shot went. Horowitz seemed to be saying that guns that are easy to fire accurately should be banned. Guns that are more accurate are better for all the constitutionally protected uses of firearms, including self-defense, hunting, and target shooting. To single them out for prohibition is misguided.

Barrel covers. For long guns that do not have a forward grip, the user may stabilize the firearm by holding the barrel with his nondominant hand. A barrel cover or shroud protects the user's hand. When a gun is fired repeatedly, the barrel can get very hot. This is not an issue in deer hunting (where no more than a few shots will be fired in a day), but it is a problem with other kinds of hunting, and it is a particular problem in target shooting, where dozens or hundreds of shots will be fired in a single session.[70]

Threaded barrel for safety attachments. Threading at the end of a gun barrel can be used to attach muzzle brakes or sound suppressors.

When a round is fired through a gun barrel, the recoil from the shot will move the barrel off target, especially for a second, follow-up shot. Muzzle brakes reduce recoil and keep the gun on target. It is difficult to see how something that makes a gun more accurate makes it so bad that it must be banned. A threaded barrel can also be used to attach a sound suppressor. Suppressors are legal in the U.S. — although buying one requires the same severe process as buying a machine gun. They are sometimes — inaccurately — called silencers. Suppressors typically reduce a gunshot's noise by about 15-20 decibels, which still leaves the gunshot louder than a chainsaw.[71]

James Bond and some other movies give the false impression that a gun with a silencer is nearly silent and is only used by professional assassins. Actually, sound suppressors are typically used by people who want to protect their hearing or to reduce the noise heard by people living close to a shooting range. Many firearms instructors choose suppressors in order to help new shooters avoid the "flinch" that many novices display because of shooting noise.

The bans on guns with grips, folding stocks, barrel covers, or threads focus exclusively on the relatively minor ways in which a feature might help a criminal and ignore the feature's utility for sports and self-defense. The reason that manufacturers include those features on firearms is because millions of law-abiding gun owners want them for entirely legitimate purposes.

Would a Ban Be Beneficial?

Connecticut banned so-called assault weapons in 1993.[72] The Bushmaster rifle used by the Sandy Hook murderer, Adam Lanza, was not an assault weapon under Connecticut law. Nor was it an assault weapon under the federal ban that was in place between 1994 and 2004.[73] Feinstein's most recent proposal would cover that particular model of Bushmaster, but it would allow Bushmaster (or any other company) to manufacture other semiautomatic rifles, using a different name, which fire just as fast, and which fire equally powerful bullets.

In order to pass the 1994 federal ban, proponents had to accept two legislative amendments. First, the ban would sunset after

10 years. Second, the Department of Justice would commission a study of the ban's effectiveness. The study would then provide members of Congress with information to help them decide whether to renew the ban or let it expire.

Attorney General Janet Reno's staff selected the researchers, who produced their final report in 2004, which was published by the Department of Justice's research arm, the National Institute of Justice. It concludes: "we cannot clearly credit the ban with any of the nation's recent drop in gun violence... . Should it be renewed, the ban's effects on gun violence are likely to be small at best and perhaps too small for reliable measurement."[74] As the report noted, assault weapons "were used in only a small fraction of gun crimes prior to the ban: about 2% according to most studies and no more than 8%."[75] Most of the firearms that were used in crime were handguns, not rifles. Recall that "assault weapons" are an arbitrarily defined set of guns. Thus, criminals, to the degree that the ban affected them at all, could easily substitute other guns for so-called assault weapons.

With respect to the ban's impact on crime, the study said that "the share of crimes involving" so-called assault weapons declined, due "primarily to a reduction in the use of assault pistols," but that that decline "was offset throughout at least the late 1990s by steady or rising use of other guns equipped with" magazines holding more than 10 rounds.[76] In other words, criminals easily substituted some guns for others.[77]

What about state-level assault-weapons bans? As noted above, Connecticut has had such a ban since 1993. Economist John Lott examined data for the five states with assault-weapon bans in his 2003 book, *The Bias against Guns*. Controlling for sociological variables, and testing the five states with bans against the other 45 states, he found no evidence of a reduction in crime. To the contrary, the bans were associated with increased crime in some categories.[78] Whether the adverse effect Lott reports is a phantom of statistical analyses or random factors, the state-level data do not support the claim that assault weapons bans reduced crime rates. The National Institute of Justice study, discussed above, also examined state and local laws, and found no statistically discernable reductions in crime or its severity.

Regarding mass murders in particular, in 2012 Mother Jones examined 62 mass shootings since 1982, finding that 35 of the 142 guns used were designated as assault weapons.[79] The Mother Jones study has been criticized for its selective and inconsistent decisions about which incidents to include. To take one example of an incident not involving an "assault weapon" that Mother Jones did not include, a man murdered 22 people at a Texas cafeteria in 1991 using a pair of ordinary semiautomatic pistols. He reloaded the guns several times.[80] Tragically, in order to comply with laws against concealed carry, Suzanna Hupp left her own handgun in her car before entering that cafeteria, rendering her defenseless as the attacker murdered her parents and many others, in circumstances when she had a clear, close shot at him while he was distracted.[81] And recall that the most deadly U.S. firearms mass murder perpetrated by a single individual was at Virginia Tech University, where the perpetrator used a pair of ordinary handguns, not assault weapons, to murder 35 people.[82]

Confiscation and Registration

The most extreme form of gun control is confiscation. The Brady Campaign, and other gun-control groups, supported a 1976 Massachusetts ballot initiative for handgun confiscation.[83] Although the proposal was rejected by 69 percent of the voters, confiscation continues to surface whenever gun-control advocates believe that it might be politically viable.[84] For example, after the December 2012 murders in Newtown, Connecticut, Governor Dannel Malloy (D-CT) created the Sandy Hook Commission to make recommendations to enhance public safety. That commission released its final report in March 2015. Recommendation No. 10 would ban the possession of "any firearm capable of firing more than 10 rounds without reloading."[85] If such a ban were in effect all across the country, it would cover tens of millions of guns already in the homes of gun owners. To avoid the criminal penalty for possession, gun owners would have to surrender their arms to the government. Malloy hedged his response to the commission's recommendation. He said there was no appetite in the legislature for such drastic proposals "at the moment."[86]

Gun Controls in Great Britain

President Obama and other gun control supporters have urged the United States to follow the policies of Great Britain and Australia, with mass confiscation of firearms.[87] Australia confiscated all semiautomatic rifles, all semiautomatic shotguns, all pump-action shotguns, and all handguns above .38 caliber. Great Britain confiscated virtually all handguns, and all semiautomatic and pump-action rifles above .22 caliber. Even nonlethal defensive arms, such as pepper sprays or stun guns, are prohibited. The President's advocacy of confiscation helps explain why constitutional-rights advocates resist the registration of guns and gun owners, since registration lists have been used for confiscation.

Great Britain's confiscation of semiautomatic rifles took place in the wake of a mass murder in 1987. The culprit murdered 16 people and wounded 14 more in an eight-hour killing spree in the small town of Hungerford.[88] Because it took a long time for anyone with a gun to arrive to stop the killer, the rate of fire from his particular guns was irrelevant. However, the British government chose to ban all semiautomatic rifles, since those had been some of the guns used by the killer.

Later, in 1998, after a known pedophile used a handgun to murder kindergarten children in Dunblane, Scotland, Parliament banned handguns. As a result, the Gun Control Network, a prohibition advocacy group, enthused that "British controls over firearms are regarded as 'the gold standard' in many countries." According to the Gun Control Network's spokesperson Gill Marshall-Andrews, "the fact that we have a gold standard is something to be proud of."[89]

Did the British ban reduce mass murders? Before and after the bans, such crimes were so rare in Great Britain that it is hard to say definitively. Great Britain is in some ways safer, and in more ways more dangerous, than the United States. The UK homicide rate tends to fluctuate between one and two per 100,000 population.[90] The U.S. homicide rate is 4.7 (as of 2011). The difference is not entirely due to guns, since the non-gun U.S. homicide rate is consistently higher than the UK total homicide rate.

The actual rates of criminal homicides in the two countries are somewhat closer than the above numbers would indicate. The U.S. rate is based on initial reports of homicides, and includes self-defense killings (about 7-12 percent of the total); so the U.S. rate would be about half a point lower if only criminal homicides were counted.[91]

The statistics from England and Wales are based only on final dispositions, so an unsolved murder, or a murder that is pleaded down to a lesser offense, is not counted as a homicide. In addition, multiple murders are counted as only a single homicide for Scottish statistics.[92] Even so, it is true that the U.S. homicide rate is higher than in the UK

In other categories of major violent crime, the UK is generally worse than the United States. In 2010, the assault rate per 100,000 population was 250.9 in the United States; 664.4 in England and Wales; 1449.7 in Scotland; and 80.6 in Northern Ireland.[93]

For robbery, the results are closer, although the UK as a whole is still worse. The U.S. rate was 115.3; England and Wales had 137.9; Northern Ireland 75.0; and Scotland 49.

Burglary rates were: United States 695.9; England and Wales, 946.1; Northern Ireland, 658.7; and Scotland, 479.1. So the overall UK burglary rate is significantly worse (considering that England and Wales contain 89 percent of the UK population, and the burglary rate is more than one-third higher than in the United States). More important, the manner in which burglaries take place in the UK is much worse.

In the United States, only a fairly small percentage of home burglaries take place when the occupants are home, but in Great Britain, about 59 percent do.[94] In surveys, American burglars say that they avoid occupied homes because of the risk of getting shot.[95]

English burglars prefer occupied homes because there will be wallets and purses with cash, which do not have to be fenced at a discount. British criminals have little risk of confronting a victim who possesses a firearm. Even the small percentage of British homeowners who have a legal gun would not be able to unlock the firearm from one safe, and then unlock the ammunition from another safe (as required by law), in time to use the gun against a criminal intruder.[96] It should hardly be surprising, then, that Britain has a much higher rate of home-invasion burglaries than does the United States.

If success is measured by a reduction in handgun crime, then the Great Britain handgun confiscation was a failure. A July 2001 study from King's College London's Centre for Defense Studies found that handgun-related crime increased by nearly 40 percent in the two years following implementation of the handgun ban.

As the King's College report noted, with passage of the Firearms Act of 1997, "it was confidently assumed that the new legislation effectively banning handguns would have the direct effect of reducing certain types of violent crime by reducing access to weapons."[97] The news media proclaimed that the "world's toughest laws will help to keep weapons off the streets."[98] Yet faster than British gun owners could surrender their previously registered handguns for destruction, guns began flooding into Great Britain from the international black market, driven by the demands of the country's rapidly developing criminal gun culture.[99] By 2009, Great Britain's handgun crime rate had doubled from the pre-ban levels.[100]

Great Britain was a much safer society in the early 20th century, when the nation had virtually no gun crime and virtually no gun control. Now it has much more of both.

Registration and Confiscation in the United States

Mass prohibitions of guns or gun components or accessories invite a repetition of the catastrophe of alcohol prohibition. Just as alcohol prohibition in the 1920s spawned vast increases in state power and vast infringements of the Bill of Rights, another domestic war against the millions of Americans who are determined to possess a product that is very important to them is almost certain to cause significant erosion of constitutional freedom and traditional liberty.[101] Legal and customary protections against unreasonable search and seizure and against invasions of privacy would all suffer.[102]

Americans are well aware that gun registration can be a tool for gun confiscation, and not just in other countries. In New York City during the mid-1960s, street crime was rising rapidly. So as a gesture to "do something," the New York City Council and Mayor John Lindsay (R) enacted long-gun registration. The per gun fee was low, just a few dollars.[103] Registration never did solve crimes, and crime continued to worsen. So in 1991, with the city becoming increasingly unlivable, Mayor David Dinkins (D) made a grand gesture of his own, convincing the City Council to enact a ban on so-called assault weapons.[104] Then, the New York police used the registration lists to conduct home inspections of individuals whose registered guns had been outlawed. The police said they were ensuring that the registered guns had been moved out of the city, or had already been surrendered to the government.[105]

In California, in 2013, only strenuous opposition finally led to the defeat of a proposed law, AB 174, which, before it was amended to cover a different subject, would have confiscated grandfathered assault weapons that had previously been registered in compliance with California state law.

Precisely because of concerns about confiscation, many Americans will not obey laws that would retroactively require them to register their guns. During the first phase of the assault-weapon panic, in 1989 and 1990, several states and cities enacted bans and allowed grandfathered owners to keep the guns legally by registering them. The vast majority of gun owners refused to register.[106]

Gun-prohibition advocates are quite correct in characterizing registration as an important step on the way to confiscation.[107] That is why Congress has enacted three separate laws to prohibit federal gun registration.[108] Obama apparently hopes to reverse federal policy with his euphemistic call for a national database of guns, and his imposition of registration for many long gun sales in the southwest border states.[109]

Yet when Canada tried to impose universal gun registration the result was a fiasco. The registration system cost a hundred times more than promised. Non-compliance was at least 50 percent, and the registration system proved almost entirely useless in fighting crime. In 2012, the Canadian government repealed the registration law and ordered all the registration records destroyed.[110]

New Zealand's Arms Act of 1983, enacted at the request of the police, abolished the registration of rifles and shotguns. Rifle registration had been the law since 1920, and shotgun registration since 1968. The New Zealand Police explained that long-gun registration was expensive and impractical, and that the money could be better spent on other police work. The New Zealand Police pointed out that the database management is an enormously difficult and expensive task, that the long-gun registration database was a mess, and that it yielded virtually nothing of value to the police.[111] Although some gun-control advocates began pushing in 1997 to revive the registry — since computers would supposedly make it work this time — the plan was rejected after several years of extensive debate and analysis.[112]

As for registration in the United States, the largest, most detailed comparative study of the effects of various firearms laws was conducted by Florida State University criminologist Gary Kleck, and published in his 1991 book *Point Blank: Guns and Violence in America*. His book was awarded the highest honor by the American Society of Criminology, the Michael Hindelang Book Award, "for the greatest contribution to criminology in a three-year period." The Kleck study examined many years of crime data for the 75 largest cities in the United States. The study controlled for numerous variables such as poverty, race, and arrest rates. Kleck's study found no crime-reducing benefits from gun registration.[113] In 2013, at the request of the Canadian Department of Justice, Kleck prepared a report that synthesized all prior research in the United States and Canada. He found registration to be of no benefit in reducing any type of firearms misuse.[114]

What Can Be Done?

When policymakers consider steps to address the problem of mass homicide, they should remember that highly publicized and emotionally wrenching events can distort our understanding of risk and what ought to be done about it. Airplane disasters, for example, get a lot of media coverage, but safety experts remind us that one is more likely to get injured in an automobile accident on the way to the airport than injured in an actual airline crash.[115] We should similarly acknowledge that mass murders are rare in the United States. The risk of dying in a mass murder is roughly the same as being killed by lightning.[116]

And because favorable trends are not considered newsworthy, many people are unaware of some very positive developments. Since 1980, the U.S. homicide rate has fallen by over half, from more than 10 victims per 100,000 population annually, to under 5 today.[117] Firearm accidents involving minors have also dropped. For children (age 0 to 14), the fatal-gun accident rate has declined by 91 percent since 1950. The annual number of such accidents has plunged from its 1967 high of 598. As of 2013, there were only 69 such accidents.[118]

These favorable trends have taken place during a period when American gun ownership has soared. In 1964, when the homicide rate was about the same as it is now, per capita gun ownership was only .45 — fewer than one gun per two Americans. In 1982, there were about .77 guns per capita (about 3 guns per 4 Americans).

By 1994, that had risen to .91 (9 guns per 10 Americans). By 2010, there were slightly more guns in America than Americans.[119]

It would be inaccurate to claim that the entire reason that crime has declined in recent decades is because Americans have so many more guns, but it would be accurate to say that having more guns is not associated with more crime. If anything, just the opposite is true. Policies that seek to stigmatize or criminalize gun ownership per se (such as a universal background check law that criminalizes loaning a gun to one's sister, as discussed above) have little to do with public safety, except to undermine it.

We must also recognize that mass murderers often spend months planning their crimes. These are generally not crimes of passion that are committed in the heat of the moment. Dylan Klebold and Eric Harris spent several months plotting their 1999 attack at Columbine High School. Dylann Roof allegedly plotted for six months prior to his attack in Charleston, South Carolina. Adam Lanza attempted to destroy the evidence of his plan to attack Sandy Hook students, but investigators uncovered the extensive research he had done on mass murders in the months leading up to that incident.

While the nature of these crimes makes absolute prevention impossible, there are, nevertheless, certain policy areas that deserve consideration. A large proportion of mass murderers — and about one-sixth of "ordinary" murderers — are mentally ill.[120] Better care, treatment, and stronger laws for civil commitment could prevent some of these crimes. The Tucson murderer, Jared Loughner, was expelled from Pima Community College because he was accurately found to be dangerously mentally ill; unfortunately, there was no follow-up. The Aurora theater murderer, James Holmes, was reported by his psychiatrist to the University of Colorado Threat Assessment Team because of his expressed thoughts about committing a mass murder. But once Holmes withdrew from the university, there was no follow-up. Newtown murderer Adam Lanza's mother was aware of his anti-social malignancy and recklessly left her firearms accessible to him.[121]

There are, of course, competing interests involved when debating the curtailment of individual rights based on mental-health screening. Any involuntary commitment must respect the Constitution, which, as applied by the Supreme Court, requires proof by "clear and convincing evidence" that the individual is a danger to himself or others in order for the person to be committed.[122] Notwithstanding some similar traits among mass shooters — young, male, alienated, intelligent — it's important to remember that those traits are present in a great many young men who never harm anyone. It is also important not to stigmatize mental health treatment to such an extent that at-risk people, along with their relatives and friends, refuse to seek help for fear of the consequences.

These are nontrivial considerations that must be weighed before any expansion of the civil commitment system. Better voluntary mental health treatment is expensive in the short run, but pays for itself in the long run through reduced criminal justice and imprisonment costs, not to mention reduced costs to victims.[123]

Unfortunately, misguided laws in recent years have made certain buildings vulnerable to sociopaths who, like Adam Lanza, aim to kill as many people as possible before there is effective resistance. By state law, Sandy Hook Elementary School was a gun-free zone: the state forbids carrying guns at schools, even by responsible adults who have been issued a permit based on the government's determination that they have the good character and training to safely carry a firearm throughout the state.[124] Thus, law-abiding adults were prohibited from protecting the children in their care, while an armed criminal could enter the school easily.

Over the last 25 years, there have been at least 10 cases in which armed persons have stopped incipient mass murder: a Shoney's restaurant in Alabama (1991); Pearl High School in Mississippi (1997); a middle school dance in Edinboro, Pennsylvania (1998); Appalachian School of Law in Virginia (2002); Trolley Square Mall in Salt Lake City (2007); New Life Church in Colorado (2007); Players Bar and Grill in Nevada (2008); Sullivan Central High

School in Tennessee (2010); Clackamas Mall in Oregon (2012; three days before Newtown); Mayan Palace Theater in San Antonio (2012; three days after Newtown); and Sister Marie Lenahan Wellness Center in Darby, Pennsylvania (2014).[125]

Gun prohibitionists insist that armed teachers, or even armed school guards, won't make a difference, but in the real world, they have — even at the Columbine shooting, where the armed school resource officer (a sheriff's deputy, in that case) was in the parking lot when the first shots were fired. The officer fired two long-distance shots and drove the killers off the school patio, saving the lives of some of the wounded students there. Unfortunately, however, the officer failed to pursue the killers into the building — perhaps due to a now-abandoned law enforcement doctrine of waiting for the SWAT team to arrive.

The contrasts are striking and tragic. The attempted massacre at New Life Church in Colorado Springs was stopped by a private citizen with a gun; the massacre at South Carolina's Emanuel AME wasn't. The mass murder at Pearl High School was stopped by a private citizen (the vice principal) with a gun; the mass murder at Newtown's elementary school wasn't stopped until the police arrived. The shootings at Appalachian Law School ended when private citizens (armed students) subdued the gunman; the shootings at Virginia Tech continued until the police arrived. More licensed-carry laws that reduce the number of pretend gun-free zones are an effective way to save lives.[126]

Conclusion

Firearms in the hands of law-abiding citizens enhance public safety. Firearms in the wrong hands endanger everyone. Responsible firearms policies focus on thwarting dangerous people and do not attempt to infringe the constitutional rights of good persons. Background checks on firearms sales can be improved by including more records on persons who have been adjudicated to be so severely mentally ill that they are a genuine threat.

Extending federal gun control to private intrastate sales between individuals — and to firearms loans among friends and family — is constitutionally dubious, and imposes severe burdens for no practical benefit. Such a system is futile without registration of all firearms. Gun owners have justifiably resisted gun registration because it has facilitated gun confiscation in the United States and other nations.

It is false to claim that common firearms are "assault weapons" and it is false to claim that common magazines are high capacity. Outlawing standard firearms and their magazines deprives innocent victims of the arms that may be best-suited for their personal defense. Sensational crimes are often used to push poorly conceived laws which criminalize peaceable gun owners. The most effective paths to preventing mass shootings are improving access to mental care and removing impediments to lawful self-defense and defense of others.

Notes

1. The author wishes to thank Ari Armstrong for his research assistance in the preparation of this paper. Quoted in Peter Baker, "After Charleston Shooting, a Sense at the White House of Horror, Loss, and Resolve," New York Times, June 18, 2015.

2. Quoted in ibid.

3. Brady Center to Prevent Gun Violence, "Charleston Families Join Brady Campaign and Members of Congress to Call for a Vote on Expanding Brady Background Checks," July 8, 2015, http://www.bradycampaign.org/press-room/charleston-families-join-brady-campaign-and-members-of-congress-to-call-for-a-vote-on.

4. Alex Seitz-Wald, "Clinton Calls for New Gun Control Laws, Outflanking Sanders," June 20, 2015, http://www.msnbc.com/msnbc/clinton-calls-new-gun-control-laws-outflanking-sanders.

5. See Richard Perez-Pena, "Problems Plague System to Check Gun Buyers," New York Times, July 27, 2015; Michael S. Schmidt, "Background Check Flaw Let Dylann Roof Buy Gun, FBI Says," New York Times, July 10, 2015.

6. James B. Jacobs, The Eternal Criminal Record (Cambridge, MA: Harvard University Press, 2015), p. 149.

7. Quoted in Ed Komenda and Jackie Valley, "What Now? Three Mass Shootings in a Week Leave Communities Wondering How to React," Las Vegas Sun, June 15, 2014.

8. Meg Wagner, "Judge Who Detained Lafayette Movie Theater Shooter John Houser Says She Couldn't Force Him into Mental Hospital: 'I Did My Job.'" New York Daily News, July 29, 2015, http://www.nydailynews.com/news/national/la-cinema-shooter-not-committed-mental-hospital-judge-article-1.2306183.

9. 18 U.S.C. § 922(g)(4).

10. Carol D. Leonnig, David Weigel, and Jerry Markon, "Gunman Had Mental Health Problems, Bitter Family Disputes, Records Show," Washington Post, July 24, 2015, http://

www.washingtonpost.com/politics/louisiana-gunman-suffered-from-mental-illness-court-documents-show/2015/07/24/798162f0-3220-11e5-8353-1215475949f4_story.html.

11. Meg Wagner, "Louisiana Movie Theater Shooter John Russell Houser Had History of Mental Illness, Praised Hitler in Online Posts," New York Daily News, July 24, 2015, http://www.nydailynews.com/news/national/la-cinema-shooter-john-houser-history-mental-illness-article-1.2303207.

12. Tim Gordon, "Oregon's New Background Check Law Begins Sunday," KGW.com, August 7, 2015, http://www.kgw.com/story/news/local/2015/08/07/oregons-new-gun-law-goes-into-effect-sunday/31305315/.

13. Larry Buchanan, Josh Keller, Richard A. Oppel Jr., and Daniel Victor, "How They Got Their Guns," New York Times, October 3, 2015, http://www.nytimes.com/interactive/2015/10/03/us/how-mass-shooters-got-their-guns.html?action=click&contentCollection=U.S.&module=MostPopularFB&version=Full&region=Marginalia&src=me&pgtype=article.

14. Glenn Kessler, "Obama's Continued Use of the Claim that 40 Percent of Gun Sales Lack Background Checks," Washington Post, April 2, 2013, http://www.washingtonpost.com/blogs/fact-checker/post/obamas-continued-use-of-the-claim-that-40-percent-of-gun-sales-lack-background-checks/2013/04/01/002e06ce-9b0f-11e2-a941-a19bce7af755_blog.html. Note also Glenn Kessler, "Clinton's Claim that 40 Percent of Guns Are Sold at Gun Shows and Over the Internet," Washington Post, October 16, 2015.

15. 18 U.S.C. § 922(d).

16. Greg Ridgeway, Summary of Select Firearm Violence Prevention Strategies, National Institute of Justice, January 4, 2013, http://www.nraila.org/media/10883516/nij-gun-policy-memo.pdf.

17. 18 U.S.C. § 922(b)(5), 923(g)(1)(A).

18. 18 U.S.C. § 923(g)(1).

19. 18 U.S.C. §§ 922(b)(5), 923(g)(1)(A).

20. See Adam Edelman, "NY SAFE Act Weapons Registry Numbers Released," New York Daily News, June 23, 2015. (Low assault-weapon registration stats suggest low compliance with SAFE Act gun control law.) Canadian gun registration is discussed in more detail below.

21. 521 U.S. 898, 938 (1997) (Thomas, J., concurring).

22. District of Columbia v. Heller, 554 U.S. 570, 626-27 (2008).

23. 18 U.S.C. §921(a)(21)(D).

24. 18 U.S.C. §§922(a), 924.

25. 18 U.S.C. § 922(t).

26. "Recordkeeping and Background Check Procedures for Facilitation of Private Party Firearms Transfers," ATF Proc. 2013-1 (March 15, 2013), https://www.atf.gov/file/4961/download.

27. Mandatory sentences are specified in 18 U.S.C. § 924.

28. David B. Kopel, "Background Checks for Firearms Sales and Loans: Law, History, and Policy," in Harvard Journal on Legislation 53 (forthcoming, 2015), http://ssrn.com/abstract=2665432.

29. Safe Communities, Safe Schools Act of 2013, S. 649, Section 122: Firearm Transfers, 113th Cong. (2013).

30. Ibid.

31. Lawrence v. Texas, 539 U.S. 558 (2003) (law against consensual sex by same-sex adults had no legitimate purpose).

32. "Los Angeles Passes Law Banning Large-Capacity Gun Magazines," New York Times, July 30, 2015.

33. The New York law originally banned magazines over 7 rounds. But in March 2013, the New York legislature "suspended" the 7-round limit, replacing it with a 10-round limit, since there are many guns for which no magazines of 7 rounds or fewer are manufactured. The law still forbids the purchase of magazines holding more than 10 rounds, and requires that magazines that hold more than 7 rounds not be loaded with more than 7 except at target ranges.

34. A clip is also a device for holding ammunition. A clip is basically a rectangular strip that holds the base of several rounds of ammunition in a line. Clips were most typically used for some rifles from the 1940s. Some people use the word "clip" incorrectly when what they mean is "magazine."

35. Public Safety and Recreational Firearms Use Protection Act, Pub. L. No. 103-322, Title XI, Subtitle A, §110105(2), 108 Stat. 1996, 2000 (1994) (Sunset Sept. 2004).

36. State of Arizona, House of Representatives, House Bill 2640 (2012), amending Ariz. Rev. Stats. § 17-231.

37. See Clayton E. Cramer, "High-Capacity-Magazine Bans," National Review, December 19, 2012, http://www.nationalreview.com/articles/336006/high-capacity-magazine-bans-clayton-e-cramer.

38. For a detailed explanation of the problem of magazine loading under stress, see the amicus brief for the International Law Enforcement Educators and Trainers Association and the Independence Institute in Peruta v. San Diego, no. 10-56971 (9th Cir., May 11, 2011), http://davekopel.org/Briefs/Peruta/Intl-Law-Enforcement-Educators-and-Trainers.pdf.

39. See Bob Parker, "How the North Hollywood Shootout Changed Patrol Arsenals," February 28, 2012, http://www.policemag.com/channel/weapons/articles/2012/02/how-the-north-hollywood-shootout-changed-patrol-rifles.aspx.

40. "The failure to reduce LCM [large capacity magazines] use has likely been due to the immense stock of exempted pre-ban magazines, which has been enhanced by recent imports," the 2004 study speculates. The study notes that millions of assault weapons and large-capacity magazines were "manufactured prior to the ban's effective date." Christopher S. Koper, Daniel J. Woods, and Jeffrey A. Roth, "An Updated Assessment of the Federal Assault Weapons Ban: Impacts on Gun Markets and Gun Violence, 1994-2003: Report to the National Institute of Justice, United States Department of Justice," University of Pennsylvania (June 2004), https://www.ncjrs.gov/pdffiles1/nij/grants/204431.pdf, p. 2.

41. Josh Sugarmann, "Drug Traffickers, Paramilitary Groups ... ," in Assault Weapons and Accessories in America, Violence Policy Center, 1988, http://www.vpc.org/studies/awadrug.htm.

42. "Third of High School Seniors Take Marijuana," News Medical, December, 22, 2012, http://www.news-medical.net/news/20121222/Third-of-high-school-seniors-take-marijuana.aspx.

43. Alicia A. Caldwell, "James Holmes' Gun Jammed During Aurora Attack, Official Says," Associated Press, July 22, 2012.

44. Will Grant, "Active Shooter Response: Lessons for Experts," Blackwater, January 6, 2013, http://blackwaterusa.com/active-shooter-response-lessons-from-experts.

45. Fyock v. City of Sunnyvale, 25 F. Supp. 3d 1267, 1275 (N.D. Cal. 2014) (noting evidence that "magazines having a capacity to accept more than ten rounds make up approximately 47 percent of all magazines owned").

46. The figure is based on over half a century of manufacturing, import, and export data recorded by the Bureau of Alcohol, Tobacco, and Firearms. The table with the annual figures is available online in chapter 12 of Nicholas J. Johnson, David B. Kopel, George Mocsary, and Michael P. O'Shea, Firearms Law and the Second Amendment (New York:

Aspen Publishers, 2013). Chapters 12-15 are available at www.firearmsregulation.org. An earlier version of this table is available in the amicus brief of the International Law Enforcement Educators and Trainers Association, et al., in District of Columbia v. Heller, 554 U.S. 570 (2008), pp. App. 13-15, http://davekopel.org/Briefs/07-290bsacreprintIntlLa wEnforcementEduc&Trainers.pdf. However, the numbers in the brief are too low because they omitted firearms imports in certain years.

47. Julie Calhoun, "S.C. Senator Pushing to Strengthen Gun Laws," WRDW.com, August 18, 2015, http://www.wrdw.com/home/headlines/South-Carolina-Senator-pushing-to-strengthen-gun-laws-322143841.html.

48. John Wagner, "Martin O'Malley: 'I'm Pissed' at Lack of Action on Gun Control," Washington Post, June 19, 2015, http://www.washingtonpost.com/news/post-politics/wp/2015/06/19/omalley-im-pissed-at-lack-of-action-on-gun-control/.

49. Some machine guns are, or may be, set to fire a certain number of rounds with one pull of the trigger. Tri-burst (three rounds) is common for many new machine guns.

50. 26 U.S.C. §§ 5801-02, 5811-12, 5821-22, 5841-54, 5861; 27 Code of Federal Regulations 478-79; Bureau of Alcohol, Tobacco, and Firearms, National Firearms Act Handbook (ATF E-Publication 5320.8; revised April 2009), https://www.atf.gov/file/58251/download.

51. 18 U.S.C. § 922(o); "National Firearms Act (NFA) — Machine Guns," http://www.atf.gov/firearms/faq/national-firearms-act-machine-guns.html.

52. Bureau of Justice Statistics, Selected Findings: Guns Used in Crime 4 (July 1995), http://www.bjs.gov/content/pub/pdf/GUIC.PDF (there are 240,000 registered machineguns); Gary Kleck, Targeting Guns: Firearms and Their Control (Hawthorne, NY: Aldine de Gryter, 1997), p. 108 (half of registered machine guns are privately owned) (citing BATF, Statistics Listing of Registered Weapons, April 19, 1989). Because the manufacture of new machine guns for sale to ordinary citizens (as opposed to government agents) was banned on May 19, 1986, and because pre-ban machine guns are therefore very valuable (so owners have every incentive to keep them in working order), the 1995 data about private machine guns are likely still valid (there are about 120,000 legally registered ones).

53. Dolf L. Goldsmith, The Devil's Paintbrush: Sir Hiram Maxim's Gun, 2nd ed. (Toronto: Collector Grade Publications, 1993).

54. See David B. Kopel, Guns: Who Should Have Them? (New York: Prometheus Books, 1995), p. 162; Defense Intelligence Agency, Small Arms Identification and Operation Guide — Eurasian Communist Countries (Washington: Government Printing Office, 1988), p. 105.

55. State of Florida, Commission on Assault Weapons, Report of May 18, 1990 (summary of March 18, 1990 meeting), p. 3. (Commission member stating that California "chose those weapons from a book of pictures.")

56. For example, the 1989 California statute outlawed the Heckler and Koch "H-93," the "SIG PE-57," and the Gilbert Equipment Company "Striker 12," none of which have ever existed. Also banned was the "Encom CM-55," which is not a semiautomatic; it is a single-shot gun with a total ammunition capacity of one.

57. Assault Weapons Ban of 2013, S. 150, 113th Congress (2013).

58. In the 97th session of the Illinois General Assembly, see House Bill 0815, House Bill 263, and Amendment #1 to Senate Bill 2899 (amendment by Rep. Eddie Acevedo).

59. Colorado Senate Bill 197 (by Sen. President John Morse); David Kopel, Testimony on SB 197 before Senate Judiciary Committee, March 4, 2013, http://youtu.be/FpzbS7XgfB8.

60. See the 2011 manufacturing data from the Bureau of Alcohol, Tobacco, and Firearms, https://www.atf.gov/file/4806/download.

61. The energy that is used to turn the cylinder of the revolver (bringing the next round into place, ready to fire) comes from the user pulling the trigger. (The trigger is mechanically linked to the cylinder, and a trigger pull performs the actions of cocking the hammer and firing a round.) Thus, the revolver does not use gunpowder energy in order to load the next round. So even though a revolver is comparable to a semiautomatic handgun in that each pull of the trigger chambers and fires one round, a revolver is a not a semiautomatic.

62. The formula is: KE = ½ MV2. Or in words: the kinetic energy is equal to one-half of the mass times the square of the velocity.

63. Rifles have longer barrels than handguns, and rifle cartridges generally burn more gunpowder. Thus, a bullet shot from a rifle spends more time traveling through the barrel than does a bullet shot from a handgun. As a result, the rifle bullet receives a longer, more powerful push from the expanding cloud of gunpowder in the barrel, so rifles generally deliver more kinetic energy than do handguns. As for shotguns, the mass of shot pellets is often heavier than any single rifle or handgun bullet, so shotguns have very high kinetic energy at short ranges. But their kinetic energy drops rapidly because the round pellets quickly lose speed because of air friction. Rifle and handgun bullets are far more aerodynamic than are shotgun pellets.

64. If the gun's caliber is .17, that means the gun's barrel is 17/100 of an inch wide and can accommodate a bullet that is very slightly smaller. So a .38 caliber bullet is bigger than a .17 caliber bullet, and a .45 caliber bullet is bigger than either of them. (Calibers can also be expressed metrically: 9 mm is nearly the same as .357 inches, which is slightly smaller than a .38 bullet). The bullet's size depends on its width (caliber) and on its length, so one .45 caliber bullet might be longer, and hence heavier, than another .45 caliber bullet. For any particular gun in any particular caliber, there are a variety of rounds available, some of which have more gunpowder than others. More gunpowder makes the bullet fly straighter for longer distances (especially important in many types of hunting or target shooting); less gunpowder reduces recoil and makes the gun more comfortable to shoot and more controllable for many people.

65. Measured at the muzzle. Kinetic energy begins declining as soon as the bullet leaves the barrel because air friction progressively reduces velocity.

66. Frank C. Barnes, Cartridges of the World: A Complete and Illustrated Reference for Over 1500 Cartridges (Iola, WI: Krause Publications, 2014).

67. Many gun manufacturers produce a single model of firearm in several different calibers. While .223 is the most common caliber for the AR-15, larger calibers are available, and some of those would be suitable for bigger game. The claim that so-called assault weapons are high-velocity is true only in the trivial sense that most guns which are called assault weapons are rifles — and rifles are generally higher velocity than handguns or shotguns.As for the handguns which are sometimes mislabeled as "assault weapons," they are lower velocity, with less powerful bullets, than the most powerful handguns. The most powerful handgun calibers, such as the .44 Magnum and .454 Casull (often carried by hikers and hunters for self-defense against bears), are mostly revolvers.

68. Bureau of Alcohol, Tobacco, and Firearms, Federal Explosives Laws and Regulations (2012), https://www.atf.gov/file/58741/download.

69. "Challenges and Implications of President Obama's Gun Control," PBS Newshour, January 16, 2013, http://video.pbs.org/video/2326406075/.

70. The types of hunting that might include enough shots in a short period to heat the barrel include pest and predator control (e.g., prairie dogs on a ranch), and wild boars.

71. A chainsaw's decibel (dB) output measured at one meter away is 105 db. See Tontechnik-Rechner, "Decibel Table — SPL — Loudness Comparison Chart," http://www.

sengpielaudio.com/TableOfSoundPressureLevels.htm. The use of a suppressor takes the dB level for a firearm down to the high 120s. That makes "silenced" firearms about 20 dB louder than a chainsaw. The decibel scale is logarithmic, not linear, so a sound 20 dB more sounds four times louder. See Steve Claridge, "How Loud Is Too Loud: Decibel Levels of Common Sounds," Hearing Aid Know, http://www.hearingaidknow.com/2007/03/how-loud-is-too-loud-decibel-levels-of-common-sounds/. For additional background, see Robert Silvers, "Results," 2005, http://www.silencertalk.com/results.htm. See also, David B. Kopel, "Silencers, gun," in Forensic Science, ed. Ayn Embar-Seddon and Allan D. Pass (Salem, MA: Salem Press, 2008); Alan C. Paulson, Silencer: History and Performance: Sporting and Tactical Silencers (Boulder, CO: Paladin Press, 1996).

72. Conn. Gen. Stats. § 53-202a-o; 1993, P.A. 93-306.

73. Jacob Sullum, "How Do We Know an 'Assault Weapon' Ban Would Not Have Stopped Adam Lanza? Because It Didn't," Reason, December 17, 2012, http://reason.com/blog/2012/12/17/how-do-we-know-an-assault-weapon-ban-wou.

74. Christopher S. Koper, Daniel J. Woods, and Jeffrey A. Roth, "An Updated Assessment of the Federal Assault Weapons Ban: Impacts on Gun Markets and Gun Violence, 1994-2003: Report to the National Institute of Justice, United States Department of Justice," University of Pennsylvania, June 2004, https://www.ncjrs.gov/pdffiles1/nij/grants/204431.pdf, p. 3.

75. Ibid., p. 2.

76. Ibid.

77. Writing for Salon, Alex Seitz-Wald objects to calling the 1994 ban a failure simply because the 2004 study showed no evidence that it did any good. Seitz-Wald believes that the ban showed "some encouraging signs" since, for example, some criminals substituted non-assault guns for assault guns. Interviewing researcher Christopher Koper, Seitz-Wald found that he agrees with speculation that if the 1994 bans had stayed in effect, they might have eventually done some good, although there was as of yet no evidence to support this hope. Alex Seitz-Wald, "Fact Check: LaPierre's Big Fib," Salon, January 30, 2013, http://www.salon.com/2013/01/30/wayne_lapierre_hopes_you_dont_read_that_study_he_mentioned.

78. John Lott, The Bias against Guns: Why Almost Everything You've Heard About Gun Control Is Wrong (Washington: Regnery Publishing, 2003), p. 207. Looking at the raw crime data, Lott observes: The comparison group here is the forty-five states that did not adopt a ban. For both murder and robbery rates, the states adopting assault weapons bans were experiencing a relatively faster drop in violent crimes prior to the ban and a relatively faster increase in violent crimes after it. For rapes and aggravated assaults, the trends before and after the law seem essentially unchanged.

Based on the crime data, Lott concludes that it is "hard to argue that ... banning assault weapons produced any noticeable benefit in terms of lower crime rates." In statistical analyses that seek to control for other possible factors in the fluctuations of crime rates, Lott finds that, if anything, the state-level assault weapons bans had an adverse effect on crime rates:

Presumably if assault weapons are to be used in any particular crimes, they will be used for murder and robbery, but the data appears more supportive of an adverse effect of an assault weapons ban on murder and robbery rates ... , with both crime rates rising after the passage of the bans.... . Murder and robbery rates started off relatively high in the states that eventually adopted a ban, but the gap disappears by the time the ban is adopted. Only after instituting the ban do crime rates head back up. There is a very statistically significant change in murder and rape rate trends before and after the adoption of

the ban.... . It is very difficult to observe any systematic impact of the ban on rape and aggravated assault rates. [See p. 214.]
See also Mark Gius, "An Examination of the Effect of Concealed Weapons Laws and Assault Weapons Ban on State-level Murder Rates," Applied Economic Letters 21, no. 4 (November 26, 2013): 265-67.

79. Mark Follman, Gavin Aronsen, and Deanna Pan, "A Guide to Mass Shootings in America," Mother Jones, December 15, 2012, http://www.motherjones.com/politics/2012/07/mass-shootings-map; see also Mark Follman, Gavin Aronsen, and Deanna Pan, "US Mass Shootings, 1982-2012: Data from Mother Jones' Investigation," Mother Jones, December 28, 2012, http://www.motherjones.com/politics/2012/12/mass-shootings-mother-jones-full-data. Mother Jones missed more than 40 percent of the cases which met its selection criteria. Nor did it consistently follow its purported selection criteria. See James Alan Fox, "Mass Shootings not Trending," Boston Globe, January 23, 2013, http://www.boston.com/community/blogs/crime_punishment/2013/01/mass_shootings_not_trending.html; Grant Duwe, "The Truth about Mass Public Shootings," Reason.com, October 28, 2014, http://reason.com/archives/2014/10/28/the-truth-about-mass-public-shootings.

80. Thomas C. Hayes, "Gunman Kills 22 and Himself in Texas Cafeteria," New York Times, October 17, 1991, http://www.nytimes.com/1991/10/17/us/gunman-kills-22-and-himself-in-texas-cafeteria.html; David B. Kopel, "Hennard, George," in Notorious Lives (Salem, MA: Salem Press, 2007).

81. Suzanna Gratia Hupp, From Luby's to the Legislature (San Antonio: Privateer Publications, 2009).

82. The killer used a .22-caliber Walther P22 handgun and a 9mm Glock 19 handgun. Reed Williams and Shawna Morrison, "Police: No Motive Found," Roanoke Times, April 26, 2007.

83. At the time, the Brady Campaign called itself the National Council to Control Handguns.

84. In The Atlantic, senior editor Robert Wright said that the assault weapons issue is a "red herring." As he points out, "there's no clear and simple definition of an assault weapon, and this fact has in the past led to incoherent regulation." Wright's preferred legislation would make it illegal to sell or possess a firearm — rifle or pistol — that can hold more than six bullets, and "illegal to sell or possess a firearm with a detachable magazine." In other words, Wright wants to ban the very large majority of handguns, and most rifles. This plainly violates the constitutional right to keep and bear arms. And even if there were no right to arms, the enforcement problems would be worse than the American experience with alcohol prohibition. Wright uses the example of the Newtown murders, noting that the criminal carried a rifle and two handguns and that he shot about 12 rounds before reaching the students. Wright supposes, "At that point, as he headed for the classrooms, he'd have six more rapid-fire bullets left, after which he'd have to reload his guns bullet by bullet." Robert Wright, "A Gun Control Law That Would Actually Work," The Atlantic, December 17, 2012, http://www.theatlantic.com/national/archive/2012/12/a-gun-control-law-that-would-actually-work/266342.But in a mass-murder scenario, a criminal would by no means be limited to three guns; he could easily carry many revolvers (or six-round semiautomatics). Like semiautomatics, double-action revolvers fire one round with each pull of the trigger. Besides that, revolvers can quickly be reloaded with speed loaders. The user does not have to put the fresh rounds into the cylinder one at a time.For more on the effective firing rates of revolvers and other types of guns, see Kopel, Guns: Who Should Have Them? pp. 164-65.

85. Final Report of the Sandy Hook Advisory Commission, presented to Dannel P. Malloy, State of Connecticut, March 6, 2015, pp. 67-68.

86. Quoted in "No Appetite for More Gun Control in Conn., Governor Says," Associated Press, March 6, 2015, http://www.nydailynews.com/news/national/no-appetite-gun-control-conn-governor-article-1.2140449.

87. "We know that other countries, in response to one mass shooting, have been able to craft laws that almost eliminate mass shootings. Friends of ours, allies of ours — Great Britain, Australia — countries like ours. So we know there are ways to prevent it." Barack Obama, presidential statement, October 1, 2015, https://www.whitehouse.gov/the-press-office/2015/10/01/statement-president-shootings-umpqua-community-college-roseburg-oregon.

88. Joyce Lee Malcolm, "Two Cautionary Tales of Gun Control," Wall Street Journal, December 26, 2012, http://online.wsj.com/article/SB10001424127887323777204578195470446855466.html.

89. House of Commons, Home Affairs, Second Report, "Controls over Firearms," Session 1999-2000, April 6, 2000, at ¶22, http://www.publications.parliament.uk/pa/cm199900/cmselect/cmhaff/95/9502.htm.

90. UN Data, "Intentional Homicide, Number, and Rate per 100,000 People," http://data.un.org/Data.aspx?d=UNODC&f=tableCode%3A1 (1.6. in 1995, rising to 2.1 in 2002, falling to 1.2 in 2009).

91. Gary Kleck, Point Blank: Guns and Violence in America (Hawthorne, NY: Aldine de Gruyter, 1991), p. 114.

92. See Joyce Lee Malcolm, Guns and Violence: The English Experience (Cambridge, MA: Harvard University Press, 2002), pp. 228-31; and Patsy Richards, "Homicide Statistics," Research Paper 99/56, House of Commons Library Social and General Statistics Section, May 27, 1999, p. 9. See also "Statistics Release: Homicides in Scotland in 2001-Statistics Published," A Scottish Executive National Statistics Publication, November 28, 2002, http://www.scotland.gov.uk/stats/bulletins/00205-00.asp, at Note 2 ("A single case of homicide is counted for each act of murder or culpable homicide irrespective of the number of perpetrators or victims.")

93. The assault, robbery, and burglary statistics are from the United Nations Office of Drugs and Crime, http://www.unodc.org/unodc/en/data-and-analysis/statistics/data.html. (For historical reasons, these three jurisdictions within the UK often keep separate crime statistics. In terms of population, England and Wales has about 56 million people, Northern Ireland fewer than two million, and Scotland about five million. Thus, England and Wales have about 90 percent of the UK population.) See "England and Wales Population Rises 3.7m in 10 years," The Guardian (London), July 16, 2012, http://www.guardian.co.uk/world/2012/jul/16/england-wales-population-rises; Scotland: The Official Gateway to Scotland, "Population of Scotland," http://www.scotland.org/about-scotland/the-scottish-people/population-of-scotland.

94. British Crime Survey, supplementary tables for 2010-2011, Table 1.8 (for 2010/11), http://www.homeoffice.gov.uk/publications/science-research-statistics/research-statistics/crime-research/nature-burglary; David B. Kopel, "Lawyers, Guns, and Burglars," Arizona Law Review 43 (2001): 345, 347, http://ssrn.com/abstract=2594535.

95. Kopel, "Lawyers, Guns, and Burglars," pp. 354-55.

96. By the late 20th century, Great Britain had one of the lowest rates of gun ownership in the Western World. Only 4 percent of British households would admit gun ownership to a telephone pollster. David B. Kopel and Joseph Olson, "All the Way Down the Slippery Slope: Gun Prohibition in England, and Some Lessons for America," Hamline Law Review 22 (1999): 399, 427, http://ssrn.com/abstract=149029.

97. "Illegal Firearms in the United Kingdom," Centre for Defense Studies, King's College London, Working Paper 1, July 2, 2001, p. 7.

98. Philip Johnston, "World's Toughest Laws Will Help to Keep Weapons off the Streets," The Telegraph, November 2, 1996.

99. "Illegal Firearms in the United Kingdom," Centre for Defense Studies, King's College London, Working Paper 4, July 2, 2001, p. 15.

100. Joyce Lee Malcolm, "The Soft-on-Crime Roots of British Disorder," Wall Street Journal, August 16, 2011 (citing Telegraph reports on government statistics from October 2009), http://online.wsj.com/article/SB10001424053111903918104576502613435380574.html.

101. David B. Kopel and Trevor Burrus, "Sex, Drugs, Alcohol, Gambling, and Guns: The Synergistic Constitutional Effects," Albany Government Law Review 7 (2013): 306-31, http://ssrn.com/abstract=2232257.

102. For a more detailed analysis of the civil rights implications of gun prohibition laws, see David B. Kopel, "Peril or Protection? The Risks and Benefits of Handgun Prohibition," St. Louis University Public Law Review 12 (1993): 285, 319-23, http://davekopel.org/2A/LawRev/lrstlupl.htm.

103. Currently codified at N.Y.C. Administrative Code § 10-304; formerly § 436-6.9, enacted by Local Law 106/1967 § 1.

104. N.Y.C. Administrative Code, § 10-301(16).

105. "Firearms Registration: New York City's Lesson," National Rifle Association, Institute for Legislative Action, January 27, 2000, http://www.nraila.org/news-issues/fact-sheets/2000/firearms-registration-new-york-city%60s.aspx?s=New+York+1991&ps= (Jeremy Travis, N.Y. Police Department deputy commissioner of legal matters, quoted in New York Daily News: "The department is taking owners at their word, but spot checks are planned.")

106. Kopel, Guns: Who Should Have Them? p. 186; Seth Mydans, "California Ends Year with Rush to Comply with Firearms Law," New York Times, January 2, 1991 (up to 20,000 persons registered grandfathered assault weapons by the California deadline of December 31, 1990, out of an estimated pool of 300,000); and Carl Ingram, "Few Takers for Assault Gun Grace Period," Washington Times, February 17, 1992 (46,000 California assault weapons registered out of an estimated pool of between 200,000 and 600,000).

107. Pete Shields, an early president of the Brady Campaign, explained in 1977: "The first problem is to slow down the number of handguns being produced and sold in this country. The second problem is to get handguns registered. The final problem is to make possession of all handguns and all handgun ammunition — except for the military, police, licensed security guards, licensed sporting clubs, and licensed gun collectors — totally illegal." Quoted in Richard Harris, "A Reporter at Large: Handguns," New Yorker, July 26, 1976, p. 58. (At the time, Shields' group was called the National Council to Control Handguns. It later changed its named to Handgun Control, Inc., and then changed again to "Brady Campaign.")

108. Stephen P. Halbrook, "Congress Interprets the Second Amendment: Declarations by a Co-Equal Branch on the Individual Right to Keep and Bear Arms," Tennessee Law Review 62 (1995): 597, 623-26.In December 1940, Congress passed the Property Requisition Act to allow the military to seize property (with compensation) for national defense needs. The Act expressly forbade the seizure or registration of citizens' firearms. The House Committee on Military Affairs explained that the language to protect the Second Amendment was added "in view of the fact that certain totalitarian and dictatorial nations are now engaged in the wholesale destruction of personal rights and liberties. H.R. Rep. No. 1120, at 2 (1941), 77th Congress, 1st sess. In a floor debate, Rep. Edwin Arthur Hall

(R-NY) stated: "Before the advent of Hitler or Stalin, who took power from the German and Russian people, measures were thrust upon free legislatures of those countries to deprive the people of the possession and use of firearms, so that they could not resist the diabolical and vitriolic state police organizations as the Gestapo, the Ogpu, and the Cheka." Cong. Rec. 87 (1941): 6811. Rep. Dewey Short (R-MO) pointed out that "The method employed by Communists in every country that has been overthrown has been to disarm the populace …" Cong. Rec. 87 (1941): 7100. Lyle Boren, an Oklahoma Democrat, cited Trotsky and Hitler as executors of the kinds of gun control that must always be resisted in America. Cong. Rec. 87 (1941): 7101.In 1986, the Firearms Owners' Protection Act became law. It forbids the creation of a federal registry of guns or gun owners. See 18 U.S. Code § 926(a). When Congress set up the National Instant Check System in 1994 it required that once a check was completed, the record of an approved sale should be destroyed. See 18 U.S. Code § 922(t)(2)(C). The Clinton administration did not obey this requirement, but the Bush administration did. See David B. Kopel, Paul Gallant, and Joanne Eisen, "Instant Check, Permanent Record," National Review Online, August 10, 2000, http://davekopel.org/NRO/2000/Instant-Check-Permanent-Record.htm.

109. By executive fiat, President Obama unilaterally imposed federal registration on anyone who buys two or more semiautomatic rifles within a one-week period in the four southwest border states. "Acting Director Announces Demand Letters for Multiple Sales of Specific Long Guns in Four Border States," Bureau of Alcohol, Tobacco, and Firearms, December 20, 2010, Agency Information Collection Activities: Proposed Collection, 75 Fed. Reg. 79,021 (Dec. 17, 2010). ATF began issuing demand letters for gun registration in July 2011.

110. 41st Parliament, 1st Session, Bill C-19, "Ending the Long-gun Registry Act," (Royal Assent received April 5, 2012), http://www.parl.gc.ca/LegisInfo/BillDetails. aspx?Language=E&Mode=1&billId=5188309; and Gary A. Mauser, "Misfire: Firearm Registration in Canada," Public Policy Sources, No. 48, Fraser Institute Occasional Paper (Vancouver, BC), 2001.

111. See David B. Kopel, The Samurai, The Mountie, and The Cowboy (Washington: Cato Institute, 1992), pp. 238-40.

112. Kelly Buchanan, "New Zealand," in Firearms-Control Regulation and Policy, Law Library of Congress, February 2013, http://www.loc.gov/law/help/firearms-control/ firearms-control.pdf, pp. 149-68.

113. Kleck, Point Blank, p. 420, Table 10.4.

114. Gary Kleck, "Expert Report on Canadian Long Gun Registration Law" (expert opinion presented to Canadian Department of Justice, September 27, 2013).

115. Ransom Stephens, "How Much Safer Is It to Fly Than Drive?" Examiner.com, January 24, 2011, http://www.examiner.com/article/how-much-safer-is-it-to-fly-than-drive-really. See also Bruce Schneier, Schneier on Security (Indianapolis: Wiley, 2008); John Mueller, "A False Sense of Insecurity," Regulation (Fall 2004): 42-46; and Aaron Wildavsky, Searching for Safety (New Brunswick, NJ: Transaction, 1988).

116. According to the FBI, there were 37 mass shooting deaths per year, on average, between 2000 and 2013. J. Pete Blair and Katherine W. Schweit, "A Study of Active Shooter Incidents in the United States Between 2000 and 2013," Texas State University and Federal Bureau of Investigation, U.S. Department of Justice (2014). According to the National Weather Service, there were 32 lightning-strike fatalities per year on average between 2006 and 2014. National Weather Service, "U.S. Lightning Deaths in 2015: 25," www.nws.noaa. gov/om/lightning/fatalities.shtml.

117. "Estimated Crime in United States — Total," U.S. Department of Justice, Uniform Crime Reporting Statistics, http://www.ucrdatatool.gov/Search/Crime/State/RunCrimeStatebyState.cfm.

118. Data available at Centers for Disease Control and Prevention, "About Underlying Cause of Death, 1999-2013," http://wonder.cdc.gov/ucd-icd10.html. Agree to the terms of data, then under option 6 on the next screen, choose "Injury Intent and Mechanism." Then choose "Unintentional" for "Injury Intent" and choose "Firearm" for "Injury Mechanism." For persons of all ages, in 2013 there were 505 deaths by "accidental discharge of firearms." This compares to 35,369 deaths that were caused by motor vehicle accidents; 38,851 deaths by accidental poisoning and exposure to noxious substances; 30,208 deaths by falls; and 3,391 deaths by accidental drowning.Some of these successes can be attributed to changes in public policy, such as greater incarceration of violent criminals. Other successes have come from private initiatives, such the NRA's Eddie Eagle gun accident prevention program for children, or the National Shooting Sports Foundation's programs to give away free gun locks.

119. Nicholas J. Johnson, David B. Kopel, Michael P. O'Shea, and George Moscary, Firearms Law and the Second Amendment: Regulation, Rights, and Policy (New York: Aspen Publishers 2012). Chapter 12 is online at http://firearmsregulation.org/FRRP_2012_Ch12.pdf.

120. Jason C. Matejkowski, Sara W. Cullen, and Phyllis L. Solomon, "Characteristics of Persons with Severe Mental Illness Who Have Been Incarcerated for Murder," Journal of the American Academy of Psychiatry Law 36 (2008): 74-86, http://www.jaapl.org/cgi/reprint/36/1/74.

121. "Danbury State's Attorney Releases Additional Information on December 14, 2012, Incident at Sandy Hook Elementary School," State of Connecticut, Division of Criminal Justice, March 28, 2013, http://www.ct.gov/csao/cwp/view.asp?a=1801&Q=521714. ("The gun locker at 36 Yogananda St. was open when the police arrived. It was unlocked and there was no indication that it had been broken into.")

122. Addington v. Texas, 441 U.S. 418 (1979).

123. David B. Kopel and Clayton E. Cramer, "Reforming Mental Health Law to Protect Public Safety and Help the Severely Mentally Ill," Howard Law Journal 58 (forthcoming, 2015), http://ssrn.com/abstract=2564680.

124. Conn. Gen. Stat. Ann. § 53a-217b (making such carry a Class D felony).

125. David B. Kopel, "Pretend 'Gun-free' School Zones: A Deadly Legal Fiction," Connecticut Law Review 42 (2009): 515, http://ssrn.com/abstract=1369783 (detailing Pearl High School, Edinboro, Appalachian School of Law, and New Life Church); Jeanne Assam, God, the Gunman, and Me (Denver: Jeane Assam Publishing, 2010); "Former Deputy Speaks On 2001 Santana High School Shooting," 10News.com, March 2, 2011, http://www.10news.com/news/former-deputy-speaks-on-2001-santana-high-school-shooting (in Santee, an off-duty officer was present while dropping off his daughter at school; he called for backup, and with an arriving officer, cornered the killer in a bathroom, where the killer was reloading); Rain Smith, "Police Officers Kill Gunman at Sullivan Central," TimesNews.net, August 30th, 2010, http://www.timesnews.net/article.php?id=9025899 (the school resource officer held the armed intruder at bay; he was shot after two more officers arrived on the scene); Rebecca Bessler, "Three Men Killed in Winnemucca Shooting on Sunday," KTVN Channel 2 News, May 25, 2008, http://www.ktvn.com/Global/story.asp?S=8378732 (Players Bar and Grill); J. Neil Schulman, "A Massacre We Didn't Hear About," Los Angeles Times, January 1, 1992 (Shoney's); Mike Benner, "Clackamas Mall Shooter Faced Man with Concealed Weapon," KGW Television, December 17, 2012, http://www.kgw.com/news/Clackamas-man-armed-confronts-mall-

We Should Be More Skeptical About Gun Control

shooter-183593571.html; and "Deputy Shoots Gunman at San Antonio Movie Theater Video," KOAI News, December 16, 2012, http://www.woai.com/articles/woai-local-news-sponsored-by-five-119078/terror-at-southwest-side-movie-theater-10644119/; Meg Wagner, "Pennsylvania Patient Who Allegedly Killed Caseworker, Shot Doctor Had 39 More Bullets, Intended Mass Shooting: DA," New York Daily News, July 25, 2014, http://www.nydailynews.com/news/national/penn-psychiatric-center-shooting-suspect-abusive-ex-wife-article-1.1880052. See also, Eugene Volokh, "Do Citizens (Not Police Officers) with Guns Ever Stop Mass Shootings?" Washington Post, October 3, 2015, https://www.washingtonpost.com/news/volokh-conspiracy/wp/2015/10/03/do-civilians-with-guns-ever-stop-mass-shootings/.

126. See Massad Ayoob, "Arm Teachers to Stop School Shootings," Wall Street Journal, May 21, 1999.

15

Fear Is a Threat to Learning

Jeffrey Alan Lockwood

Jeffrey Lockwood is Professor of Natural Sciences and Humanities Director of the MFA Program in Creative Writing at the University of Wyoming. He teaches environmental ethics and philosophy of ecology in the Philosophy Department, as well as creative writing workshops in environmental writing.

Open carry on university campuses is intended to protect students and personnel. The idea is that students have the right to safety. Many agree that universities should indeed be "safe spaces," but that the term refers to thoughts and experiences. The classroom should be a place where everyone feels safe to express their views and opinion, because that is fundamental to learning. But where does physical safety enter into it? Even if the presence of guns is effective in counteracting other potential physical threats, at what cost is this safety achieved? Is everyone—student and teacher alike—constantly on edge knowing that at any point they could be shot? Or is it simply something to adapt to? Students have the right to learn without fear, and they have the right to reach their potential without killing or being killed.

As a rational academic, living in one of the most conservative states, where legislators are planning to allow firearms in virtually all public places, including the University of Wyoming, I have labored to understand my own deep antipathy to the idea of my students and colleagues being armed.

Gun advocates and opponents can each fire off statistics; however, the debate will not be resolved with data when the fundamental conflict is a matter of ideals. I could dredge up statistics about the frequency of gun accidents, while advocates could offer numbers showing that people with concealed gun permits rarely shoot innocent bystanders.

But dueling spreadsheets fail to get to the heart of the issue. Rather, my resistance to a well-regulated militia crossing the quad between classes is rooted in non-quantifiable principles.

Fear undermines classroom learning environment

The proliferation of virtual courses notwithstanding, the soul of a university remains its classrooms. These are the places of genuine human engagement, debate, thought, and passion. Students must come prepared -— ready to learn (by having done the reading), ready to argue (by thinking critically about ideas), and ready to change (by cultivating intellectual humility).

Here they are tested and challenged. This is where they flounder and flourish. Arming students seems inimical to learning. The presence, even the possibility, of a loaded weapon casts a pall over classroom discussion.

Fear undermines the openness and vulnerability necessary for learning. When getting ready for class means preparing to die (or to kill), an academic community has failed.

I remember going back home to Albuquerque – a city with a violent and property crime rate well above the national average– for Christmas when our kids were little to find that my parents had installed burglar bars in their windows. I was overwhelmed by a sense of sadness that the city of my youth had failed so miserably that the people barricaded their homes.

Universities are meant to be safe spaces

My parents were free to live behind bars to protect their property, and the legislature wants to free me to arm myself in the classroom to guard my life. Somehow, these don't feel like liberties. I want to work at a university that is big enough to provide students with a hundred opportunities and small enough to notice one anguished student.

Maybe I'm safer if a student in my seminar is carrying a gun. For that matter, maybe I'd be safer if I wore a Kevlar vest while lecturing. But I don't want to teach where we prepare to shoot and be shot. I don't want to be a part of failure. In all likelihood, no armed student will take (or save) my life. But the same cannot be said of that student's life.

Suicide rates are already high

Suicide rates on college campuses are appalling. I said that numbers wouldn't resolve the issue, but the fact is that suicide rates among young adults has tripled since the 1950s, having become the second most common cause of death among college students. Given current statistics, the University of Wyoming with an enrollment of 14,000 can expect at least two thousand of these students to contemplate suicide, two hundred to make an attempt, and perhaps two to succeed.

I was the first person to arrive on the scene of two suicide attempts when I was in college. I mopped up a lot of blood, but razor blades are not all that effective. Guns work much better. Filled with shame, my friends asked me to hide the evidence and lie in the emergency room. I did.

They were both extremely intelligent young men. But laboring under enormous stress and failed relationships, on a dark, lonely night, collapsed into a moment of utter despair. Lonely but not alone — nearly half of all university students report symptoms of depression.

Enough of the numbers. Consider this simple statement from a college athlete who was battling depression: "If I'd had a gun, I'd have probably put a bullet in my head."

Campus grounds are not for killing or being killed

Perhaps my perspective is darkened by experience, but my deepest fear is not that a student with a gun comes to my classroom in the morning, but that the student leaves his dorm room in a body bag that evening.

Campuses are places fraught with doubt, conflict, angst, disorientation, and drama. A university education is not easy intellectually — or existentially. College is where assumptions die, identities expire, and beliefs perish. But this should not become a place where students come to kill or be killed.

A university should be where the dying dream of being an engineer is resurrected as a graphic artist, where an identity as a straight Christian gives way to being a gay ethicist, and where the parental narrative of being a biology teacher is reborn as a student's own aspiration of becoming a doctor.

But once the trigger is pulled, there will be no artist, philosopher, or doctor. Maybe I'm an idealist, but how else does one avoid cynicism and fatalism? If we aren't willing to imagine and risk, then there's no "good fight" left in the professoriate. An academic life worth living requires courage, hope, defiance and compassion. It does not require guns.

Organizations to Contact

The editors have compiled the following list of organizations concerned with the issues debated in this book. The descriptions are derived from materials provided by the organizations. All have publications or information available for interested readers. The list was compiled on the date of publication of the present volume; the information provided here may change. Be aware that many organizations take several weeks or longer to respond to inquiries, so allow as much time as possible.

The Campaign to Keep Guns Off Campus
PO Box 658
Croton Falls, NY 10519
914.629.6726
email: andy@keepgunsoffcampus.org

The Campaign to Keep Guns off Campus works with colleges and universities across the country to oppose legislative policies that would force loaded, concealed guns on campuses. Since 2008, The Campaign to Keep Guns off Campus has helped stop campus carry legislation in 18 states, and are the only national organization of its kind tasked to protect higher educational institutions and the communities they serve.

Center For Gun Policy and Research at Johns Hopkins
615 N. Wolfe Street
Baltimore, MD 21205
email: alsamuel@jhsph.edu

website:http://www.jhsph.edu/research/centers-and-institutes/johns-hopkins-center-for-gun-policy-and-research/

The Johns Hopkins Center for Gun Policy and Research is dedicated to reducing gun-related injuries and deaths through the application of strong research methods and public health principles. Its faculty have pioneered innovative strategies for reducing gun violence, and achieved a national reputation for high-quality, policy-relevant research.

Coalition To Stop Gun Violence
805 15th Street NW, Suite 502
Washington, DC 20005
(202) 408-0061csgv@csgv.org
website: http://csgv.org/

The Coalition to Stop Gun Violence seeks to secure freedom from gun violence through research, strategic engagement and effective policy advocacy.

Concealed Nation
518-407-5CCW
email: info@concealednation.org
website: http://concealednation.org/Description

Having its start in January 2013, Concealed Nation has grown to the largest concealed carry website in the world. Our primary focus of promoting responsible concealed carry has helped many on their journey to successfully implementing the carrying of firearms into their daily lives.

Crime Prevention Research Center
(484) 802-5373
email: johnrlott@crimeresearch.org
website: http://crimeresearch.org/about-us/

The Crime Prevention Research Center (CPRC) is a research and education organization dedicated to conducting academic quality research on the relationship between laws regulating the ownership or use of guns, crime, and public safety; educating the public on the results of such research; and supporting other organizations, projects, and initiatives that are organized and operated for similar purposes. It has 501(C)(3) status, and does not accept donations from gun or ammunition makers or organizations such as the NRA or any other organizations involved in the gun control debate on either side of the issue.

Everytown For Gun Safety
646-324-8250
http://everytown.org/contact-us/
website: http://everytown.org

Everytown is a movement of Americans working together to end gun violence and build safer communities. Gun violence touches every town in America. For too long, change has been thwarted by the Washington gun lobby and by leaders who refuse to take common-sense steps that will save lives.

Gun Owners of America
8001 Forbes Pl Suite 102
Springfield, VA 22151
703-321-8585
website: http://gunowners.net/cgi-bin/ttx.cgi?cmd=newticket

Described by Rand Paul as the "only no compromise gun lobby in Washington", the GOA includes action alerts and other resources for those gun enthusiast opposing any and all common sense restrictions on gun ownership and use.

Law Center To Prevent Gun Violence
268 Bush Street #555
San Francisco, CA 94104
415-433-2062
email: info@smartgunlaws.org
website: http://smartgunlaws.org/

Founded in the wake of the July 1, 1993, assault weapon massacre at 101 California Street in San Francisco that left eight dead and six wounded, the Law Center to Prevent Gun Violence is now the premier resource for legal expertise and information regarding state and federal firearms laws.

National Rifle Association
11250 Waples Mill Road
Fairfax, VA 22030
(800) 672-3888
website: https://home.nra.org/

The National Rifle Associate (NRA) is widely recognized today as a major ideological player within the conservative right. The organization is a steadfast defender of Second Amendment rights, and also provides educational materials about firearms and gun safety.

Students For Concealed Carry
website: http://concealedcampus.org/Description

Students for Concealed Carry is a student-run, national, non-partisan organization which advocates for legal concealed carry on college campuses in the United States as an effective means of self-defense.

Bibliography

Books

Saul Cornell, *A Well Regulated Militia*. Oxford, UK: Oxford UP, 2014.

Laurie DiMauro, *Gun Control: Restricting Rights or Protecting People?* Detroit, MI: Gale Cengage Learning, 2013.

Stephen Halbrook, *Gun Control in the Third Reich: Disarming the Jews and "Enemies of the State."* Independent Institute, 2013.

Noel Merino, *Gun Violence*. Farmington Hills, MI: Greenhaven Press, 2015.

Robert Spitzer. *Guns Across America*. Oxford, UK: Oxford UP, 2015.

Angela Valdez and John E. Ferguson, *Gun Control*. New York, NY: Chelsea House, 2012.

Daniel Webster Ed., *Reducing Gun Violence in America*. Baltimore, MD: Johns Hopkins UP, 2013.

Philip Wolny, *Gun Rights: Interpreting the Constitution*. New York, NY, NY: Rosen Publishing Group, 2015.

Periodicals and Internet Sources

"Appeals court rules no constitutional right to carry concealed guns," Fox News, June 9, 2016. http://www.foxnews.com/politics/2016/06/09/court-no-right-to-carry-concealed-weapons-in-public.html

John Burnett, "Does Carrying A Pistol Make You Safer?" April 12, 2016. http://www.npr.org/2016/04/12/473391286/does-carrying-a-pistol-make-you-safer

"Gun Control," Just Facts. http://www.justfacts.com/guncontrol.asp

"Handguns In America And The Rise Of The 'Concealed-Carry Lifestyle,'" Fresh Air, June 23, 2016. http://www.npr.org/2016/06/23/483211713/handguns-in-america-and-the-rise-of-the-concealed-carry-lifestyle

Kevin Michalowski, "What Kind of People Carry Concealed?" US Concealed Carry, March 13, 2015. https://www.usconcealedcarry.com/kind-people-carry-concealed/

Adam Nagourney and Erik Eckholm, , "2nd Amendment Does Not Guarantee Right to Carry Concealed Guns, Court Rules," New York Times, June 9, 2016. https://www.nytimes.com/2016/06/10/us/second-amendment-concealed-carry.html?_r=0

Michael Newbern, Johns Hopkins Report on Campus Carry Is Seriously Flawed," November 1, 2016. http://concealedcampus.org/2016/11/johns-hopkins-report-on-campus-carry-is-seriously-flawed/

Adam Winkler, "Why the Supreme Court Won't Impact Gun Rights," The Atlantic, June 7, 2016. https://www.theatlantic.com/politics/archive/2016/06/why-the-supreme-court-wont-restrict-gun-rights/485810/

Index